Theme of the Week

by
Lisa Rogulic-Newsome

illustrated by Kathryn Hyndman

Cover by Kathryn Hyndman

Copyright © Good Apple, 1991

ISBN No. 0-86653-602-7

Printing No. 98765432

Good Apple
1204 Buchanan St., Box 299
Carthage, IL 62321-0299

SIMON & SCHUSTER *A Paramount Communications Company*

Dedication

This book is fondly dedicated to my husband, John, for without his hard work and wonderful ideas, this book would never have been accomplished; and to my caring parents, John and Louise, for all their support and love.

GA1321

Table of Contents

GA1321

GA1321

v

GA1321

"Something More Than Ever Before"

by Lisa Rogulic-Newsome

We, the educators of the quote "modern child,"
Are given the task of inspiring our youth
To create and eventually think
Entirely on their own.
If we are to achieve success
In the education of <u>all children,</u>
To the fullest possible extent,
Then we need more than ever before.
We need the equipment to motivate,
To relate,
And to integrate our lives
With those of our students.
We need to get down to their level,
To learn of their interests,
Their desires,
And even their dreams.

Perhaps we need to find or rediscover
The child in ourselves.
Only then can we see through their eyes,
Hear through their ears.
And feel through their fingers,
<u>As well as their hearts.</u>

They have always maintained that
Today's youth hold the key to the future.
This is true . . .
To a certain point.

I believe that whether be it in
A public or private institution
Or whether it takes place outside the educational system per se,
It is <u>we</u>
As teachers
Who control that key.
For after all,
Is it not through our teaching,
Our loving and our sharing
That we mold and shape and direct those children
Into the adults they eventually become?

We are given so much responsibility,
We have so many outside influences
With which to compete
We must do something special,
Something more than ever before.

We must provide that little
Extra something
That makes each and every day
A worthwhile experience—
Something to talk about,
Something to remember,
Something that becomes a part of one,
Something more than ever before.

GA1321

A Word to the Wise

During the course of the school year, certain weeks can seem dry and uneventful. Wouldn't it be wonderful if you had a resource you could turn to that would spice up the time and add hours of supplemental enrichment to your class?

Well, now you've found it! Thirty-nine weeks of incredible, interesting and inspiring topics augmented with activities of every kind—science, social studies, math, language arts, creative thinking, brainstorming, creative problem solving and creative writing. *Theme of the Week* is a week-by-week calendar of themes focusing on the child, the teacher and the class.

Use the themes in the order they are presented or mix and match them to fit your needs. It's guaranteed that no week ever has to be dull again. Use *Theme of the Week* and you are in for a lot of pleasant surprises!

GA1321

Let's Speak and Not Be Meek . . . Here's How to Use *Theme of the Week*

Planning the Week

First select a topic which you feel you and your students will enjoy.

Then once a topic has been selected, spark interest in the topic by presenting Setting the Stage, found at the top of the Teacher Tactic's page. Note: Pay special attention to the topics in the table of contents that are designated for specific weeks. For example, National Newspaper Week, National Library Week and National Stamp Collecting Week are specifically dated weeks.

Next spend the middle of the week working on class projects, student work, reproducibles and various class activities which might include theme bulletin boards, theme murals or the creation of a class theme center.

The final culmination of the theme week might include individual student project presentations and possibly a theme party, where everyone brings something to add.

Teacher Tactics

These are teacher-directed activities and are chosen by the teacher.

Setting the Stage at the top is to alert students that a new topic or theme is going to be presented and, in addition, to spark interest in the theme.

Absolutely Adaptable Activities

These are student-directed activities and can be independent study, student projects or extra research and can possibly be done in small groups.

Centers

Centers are like clothing. They are suited to the needs and desires of the person using them. If you wish to create a simple center, clear off a space on a table or desk in a corner of your classroom. Cover it with colored butcher paper that matches the theme and possibly make theme letters to go over the center. Go to the library and check out a few books related to the theme and leave them in the center. And that's all there is to it. Unfinished projects can be left at the center, too.

GA1321

But if you want a much more elaborate center and one that you can keep from year to year, search through gift wrap stores for a gift wrap that matches your theme. Then cover a box with the gift wrap and hang a few simple curtain hooks on it. Create task cards in the shape of something on cards and hang them on the curtain hooks. Also, matching letters can be made from gift wrap. You will have a perfectly color-coded center that will attract students for a long time to come.

Brainstorming

Brainstorming can be done individually, in small groups or with the whole class. A topic is presented, one student gives an idea, then the next student and so on. No one should monopolize the brainstorming. If a student is doing it independently, allow him quiet time to think and list his ideas.

Researching

When an activity states *Research,* it means for the student to go to the school or public library, and check out a book(s) which pertains to the topic. He is then to open up the book(s) and try to pinpoint the paragraphs or pages that answer the activity question. Finally, the student is to paraphrase the information and answer the question.

Other sources besides books from libraries should be encouraged. Sources like parents, relatives, adult friends and specialists found in the telephone book are all possible sources of information.

Class Discussions

Before you begin a class discussion, make sure to lay down the ground rules. No one should be able to dominate the discussion, and everyone's ideas should be acknowledged. Some helpful class rules are
  1. All ideas are right—no ideas are wrong.
  2. No one's ideas should be laughed at.
  3. No one's ideas are stupid.
  4. No ideas are to be repeated—so students need to listen carefully.
  5. Present only ideas that are acceptable for school—student language needs to be acceptable.

Problem Solving

- State the problem.
- Generate solutions.
- Narrow down the solutions.
- Vote on the best solutions (up to five).
- Use the criteria to make final judgements.
- Choose the best solution based on all the information.

GA1321

Videotapes

- Tape shows off PBS and other channels, but be sure to check with your local stations for copyright laws.
- Check out tapes from your public library.
- Check out or purchase tapes from video stores.
- Always preview the tape prior to showing.
- Ask students to make a list of important facts as they are watching the video.

Guest Speakers

- Plan for the speaker well in advance.
- If you don't know one personally, use the telephone book.
- Arrange your questions ahead of time and plan on who will ask each of the questions.
- Ask students to take notes during the lecture. In the case of younger students, have them write down important words they hear by sounding them out.
- After the speaker has left, ask your students to write down what they learned.
- Write thank-you notes to the speaker.

Field Trips

- Plan a field trip at least one month in advance.
- Make each field trip educational by asking students to either carry a clipboard and take notes or hold a contest when they return to class to see who learned the most. Make sure students are accountable for what they have seen.

Role Playing

- If you'd like to plunge students head first into some of these theme weeks, try a little role playing.
- Ask students to pretend they are back in the past (as in the "Wild, Wild West") or are going into space (as in "Out of This World Week") or whatever, and they actually have become the people of the time.
- Ask students to ad-lib a conversation that might have occurred in that time.
- Discuss the conversation after it is given to determine its "authenticity."

Broken Any World Records Lately? Week

Teacher Tactics

Setting the Stage: Prior to starting this theme, pose this to your class: "Have you ever thought about participating in an event and doing so well that you might break a world's record? Perhaps something physical like running the quarter mile (.40 km) in 30 seconds or eating the most hot fudge sundaes? Well, this week we'll be discussing world records and some of the different people who made them."

The German solar probe, *Helios B,* launched in 1976 has been recorded at 149,125 mph (240,091.25 km/h). Ask your class to imagine they had a rocket that could go that speed, and they could go any place they wanted. In addition, ask students to create a map of their adventures through the universe.

The English language contains about 490,000 words, but it's doubtful whether anyone uses more than 60,000. Ask students to design their own twenty-word language, both written and spoken, and then ask each student to share his "new" language with the class.

The greatest amount of money ever found and returned was $500,000.00 in 1972. Ask your students to write an essay in which they answer the question, "If you found $500,000.00, what would *you* do?"

Tell students that the smallest independent country in the world is the state of the Vatican City, an enclave in the city of Rome. Ask them to imagine that they have been given a country of their own. Make sure they give its name, location, imports and exports, national anthem, flag, population, size, culture, customs, cities, history, etc.

Pose this statement to the class: A 100-ton (90 t) snowman was built in Schaumburg, Illinois, in 1986. List as many other uses for snow as possible.

GA1321

Broken Any World Records Lately? Week

Absolutely Adaptable Activities

The largest zipper in the world is 2074 feet (622.2 m) long. Imagine ten things it could zip and share them with the class (like someone's large mouth or the Mississippi River).

You just broke a world's record. Which one was it?

The most fattening sundae ever made weighed 33,616 pounds (15,127.2 kg) and had 30,000,000 calories. If you made a sundae like this in your backyard, what would you do? Write a sentence or a poem answer.

The biggest cake ever made weighed 90,000 pounds (40,500 kg) and was 8800 feet (2640 m) long. Imagine you had this cake at your birthday party, and it fed 300,000 people. Plan your party, complete with invitations, decorations, guest list, entertainment, etc.

A world's record is like _____. Breaking a world's record feels like _____. Name a world's record you might like to break.

The Sears Tower in Chicago, Illinois, is the tallest building in the world. Imagine you are on the roof and there is a giant cushioned trampoline-like device on the ground below. As you jump, several thoughts run through your mind. Write them down as they come to you.

The most valuable fish ever was a Russian sturgeon, caught and weighed in at 2706 pounds (1217.7 kg). It yielded 541 pounds (243.45 kg) of high quality caviar valued at $184,500.00. Write a fish story about "the big one that got away!"

An ostrich egg can be *so* big (6" to 8" [15.24 to 20.32 cm] long and 4" to 6" [10.16 to 15.24 cm] in diameter) that it can support the weight of a 380-pound (171 kg) man. Imagine that you were given one of those eggs at Easter, filled with surprises. Make a list of things you'd like to see filling it up.

Every time you see the word *world* on this page, underline it twice. Every time you see the word *was* on this page, circle it.

The largest tomato plants ever grown produced 1368 pounds (615.5 kg) of fruit. A 612-pound (275.4 kg) pumpkin was grown in 1984. A baby cucumber weighed in at 37½ pounds (16.875 kg) in 1985. Imagine that all fruits and vegetables grow to these extremes. What would a garden look like?

If you're interested in surfing, listen to this! The highest instrumentally measured wave was calculated to be 86 feet (25.8 m) high! Imagine that you are surfing along and this wave catches up to you! Write your diary entry for the day of this occurrence.

Katemfe are the plants which put out the sweetest known substance, much sweeter than sugar. Imagine something sweeter than sugar! If you had access to katemfe, create ten benefits or new uses for it.

2

GA1321

An Unlikely Match!

The tallest human ever was an 8 foot (243.84 cm), 11.1-inch (28.2 cm) man, and the shortest human was a woman who was 23.2 inches (59 cm) tall as an adult. Write an imaginary love story between these two individuals. What special problems would they face?

3

GA1321

Create a Video Game!

The highest score ever on the video game Pac-Man was 3,155,320; Ms. Pac-Man 874,530; and Super Pac-Man 855,940. Design your own video game below, complete with pictures and rules. Be as detailed as possible.

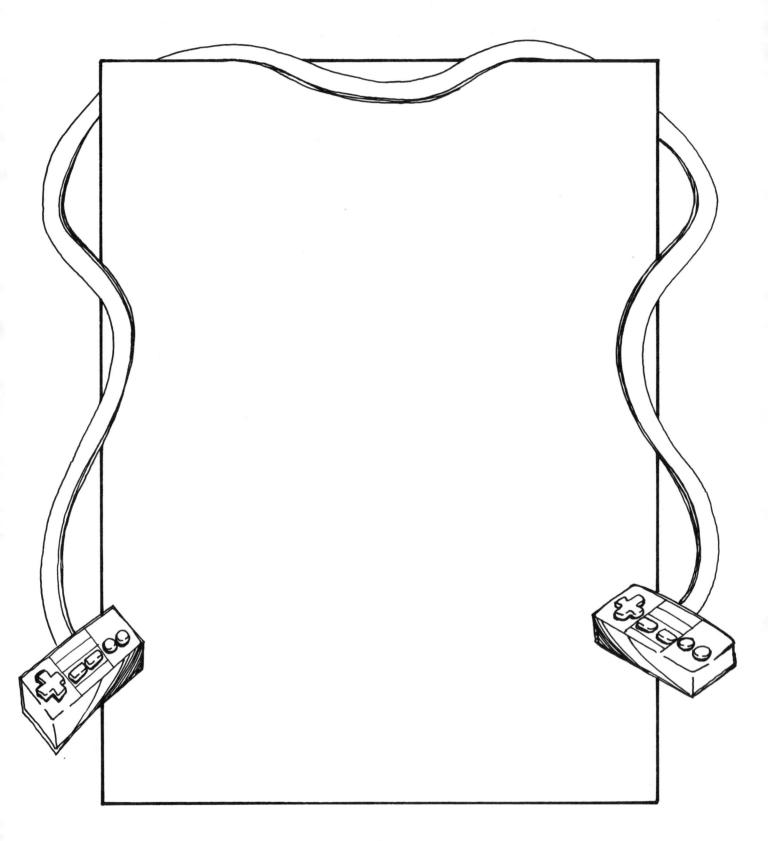

GA1321

Keep Cool!

In 1917, Death Valley, California, reported temperatures over 120° F (49° C) for forty-three consecutive days!

List all of the things you would do to keep cool were you alive at that period of time in Death Valley.

1.

2.

3.

4.

5.

6.

7.

8.

9.

10.

11.

12.

13.

14.

15.

Just the Bear Facts Week

Teacher Tactics

Setting the Stage: Prior to starting this theme, pose this to your class: "Have you ever heard of a big white bear that lives in the Arctic and has black skin? How about the brown bear that roams Yellowstone Park? Well, this week, I'll be sharing with you information about many different kinds of bears, so listen up!"

Bear is a fairly rhymable word. Hold a class contest to see how many words each student can rhyme with bear.

Polar bears are really strong swimmers and can swim for more than a hundred miles (161 k) without stopping for a rest. Pretend that your city is surrounded by the Arctic Ocean and you can swim one hundred miles (161 k) in all directions. Pin up a large map of your state and those states surrounding it. Have your class mark all those cities (or just big cities) within the hundred-mile (161 k) radius. Discuss those cities it would only take approximately two hours to reach by car.

Locate a book which depicts new baby polar bears being born. Ask the class to describe the world through the polar bear's eyes at birth, one month, two months, three months and four months of age.

If you'd like to have your class know more about how you can help to protect the polar bears, write to the World Wildlife Fund, 1601 Connecticut Ave., N.W., Washington, D.C. 20009.

Ask your class to research some of the more commonly known bears and learn how they move. Then put on a creative dramatics display where different groups of kids act out the movements of specific bears.

Bears are related to dogs, wolves and foxes, and if you look at a bear's skeleton, you can see the resemblance. Have your class create mini encyclopedias with all the animals in the bear, wolf and fox families, with similarities and differences noted.

In 1902, President Roosevelt refused to shoot a black bear while out hunting. Something very popular came out of this incident. See if someone in your class can find out what it was, and report back to the class. (Teddy bears!)

GA1321

Just the Bear Facts Week

Absolutely Adaptable Activities

Why do you think it's important to talk about bears?

Like the panda bear and the koala bear, the polar bear lives alone after it is full grown. Write about a day in the life of a solitary giant white polar bear. Think about where it goes, what it does, what other animals it encounters and how it spends its time.

Polar bears live in the Arctic Ocean, along with many other animals. Make a list of all the different animals who live around and about the polar bear.

Which bear is your favorite? Why?

Polar bears are predators and hunt smaller animals for their food. Make a list of all those animals the polar bear might want for his lunch.

Hunting a polar bear alone is a sign of courage in the Arctic. If you were faced with this challenge, what method of conquest would you choose? Write about it!

If you could have one bear for a pet, which would it be?

Imagine that a black bear was loose in your neighborhood. Outline the new security system you would design for your home and your family.

If you feel like learning more about one of the many different bears, write a report complete with illustrations of perhaps one of these bears: Alaskan brown bear, Malayan sun bear, Asiatic black bear, grizzly bear, spectacled bear and the sloth bear.

Prepare a "Bear Facts Dictionary," in which you define the following bear terms: *boar, sow, cub, plantigrade walk, predator, hibernation, "top bear," "grizzled," extinction* and *migration.*

"Black bears aren't always black." "Polar bears have black skin." Make a list of all the interesting facts you can find about the different kinds of bears.

If you were a bear, which one would you be? Why?

Research the city of Bern, Switzerland, illustrate their flag, what their coat of arms means and what the word *Bern* stands for.

Underline the word *bear* every time you find it on this page.

The sun bear especially loves honey and doesn't even mind eating the bees along with it! Write and illustrate a magazine advertisement with a sun bear as your celebrity endorser.

The grizzly is named for the grey or "grizzled" tips of its hair. If humans were named in the same fashion (after their hair), what might some of their names be?

GA1321

A Bearabunch of Questions

1. What might an Alaskan Brown Bearamunga eat for a snack?

2. How do Malayan Sun Bearettes keep cool in the hot summertime?

3. Where does a Grizzly Bearawhawho ride his horse in the Wild, Wild, West?

4. Who can an Asiatic Black Bearasaurus turn to for advice?

5. When does a Sloth Bearess become a real beauty queen?

6. Why do Spectacled Bearmonstrosities hang around small ants?

7. How does a Sun Beararoni get dressed for a ball?

8. Who comes to a Honey Beara's birthday party?

9. When does a Himalayan Bearoops get his driver's license?

10. What attracts Moon Bearettes to the moon?

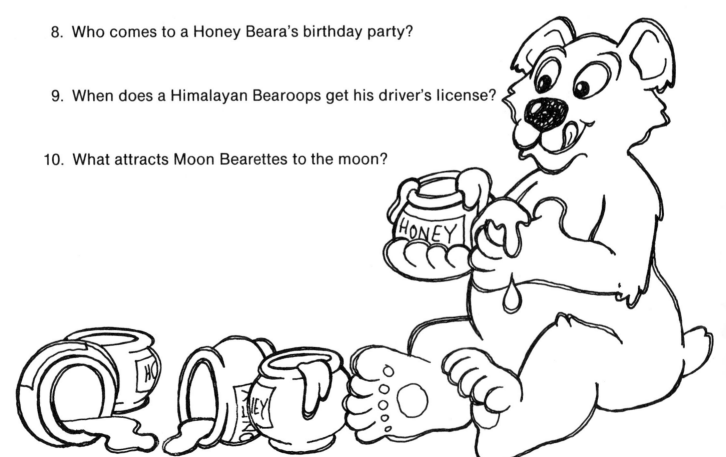

GA1321

Bear Titles to Try

Choose one of the following titles to help inspire you to write a one or two-page story. Make it "beary" good!

Sun Bears Eat Wheaties and Grow!

A Lone Spectacled Bear Cries Real Tears

Five Sloth Bears Sing Songs

Paully Polar Bear Saves the Town

Allen Asiatic Black Bear Runs Away from Home

An Alaskan Brown Bear Believes He Can Fly

Salvatore Sun Bear Sunbathes Supernaturally

The Pirate Polar Bear Raids the Seas

A Green Grizzly Groaned Very Softly

Sloth Bears Don't Slip into Suits

Honey Bears Love Munching on Bees

A Special Spectacled Bear Wins a Trophy

Polar Bears Prove to Be Princes

GA1321

A Problem Named Pinkey the Polar Bear

Specific Instructions:

A polar bear named Pinkey has escaped from the zoo and has hidden out in an ice-cream freezer. After you have heard the specific data, your job will be to brainstorm some possible solutions. The problem is, how to remove the polar bear safely, without any harm to it or the ice-cream freezer.

Data:

- One afternoon while feeding the polar bears, a zookeeper accidently left the polar bear cage unlocked and one polar bear, Pinkey, escaped from the zoo unnoticed.
- When the polar bear started meandering down the street, cars panicked and there were several traffic jams.
- One of the vehicles which stopped was a large ice-cream truck, and the back doors flew open when the ice-cream truck skidded to a stop.
- Pinkey, upset at all the traffic and noise, ran for shelter in the only place he could find—the back of the ice-cream truck.
- Pinkey is a dangerous animal and will attack a human if cornered.
- The ice-cream truck is worth $75,000 dollars, since it has some very modern new freezers and a new exterior.

Brainstorm:

Your job, in small groups, is to brainstorm every single solution possible, no matter how far out or seemingly unreal. Every idea is acceptable. All solutions will be listed on the board. Each student then will vote for the five best solutions.

Criteria:

A. Safety for Pinkey
B. Safety for the ice-cream truck
C. Safety for human life
D. Safety for other automobiles

Number Values:

5 Great Idea
4 Good Idea
3 Average Idea
2 Poor Idea
1 Not possible

Solutions

	A	B	C	D

Criteria

GA1321

Pretty as a Picture Week

(First Roll Film Camera Day, September)

Teacher Tactics

Setting the Stage: Pose the following to your class: "Is anyone in here a camera buff? Has everyone had the opportunity, sometime in his life, to take a picture with a camera? If not, maybe I can get a camera and we can take some pictures. This week we are going to discuss photography and some terms that go with it."

An invention was designed in 1884 by a man named George Eastman, and it created long rolls of photographic paper. In addition to making the "Brownie" box camera a household word, it also made photography less expensive. The first true photograph taken was by Joseph Niépce in 1824 in France.

If you need a place to go for inexpensive classroom cameras (for film and a sample camera), send a letter to:
> Power Sales Company
> Box 113
> Willow Grove, PA 19090

Contact a professional photographer to come and visit your class.

For a really creative art project, ask your students to cut out pictures of people's faces, animals' bodies and other photographed objects. Then cut each of those pictures into vertical strips. Paste on white background with strips about ½" (1.25 cm) apart. Use on your walls or bulletin boards. Ask students to name their creations.

Careers in photography might be interesting. If you'd like to learn more, write to:
> Photo Information
> Eastman Kodak Company
> 343 State Street
> Rochester, NY 14650

and ask for a free copy of *A Survey of Photographic Instruction.*

GA1321

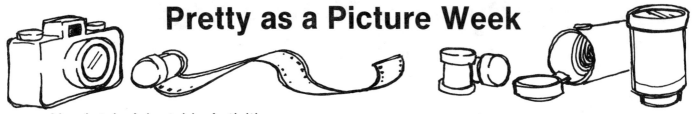

Pretty as a Picture Week

Absolutely Adaptable Activities

Compare and contrast the different popular brands of cameras on the market. Make price and quality checks and notice how sturdy they are. Make a comparison chart.

In a "Photography Extra," define the following: *negative, prints, developing, lens, underexposed, overexposed, exposure, shutter, panning, focus control* and *film cartridge.*

Write a story about you, as a photographer traveling all around the world and clicking pictures.

Leonardo da Vinci drew diagrams of a device he called a "darkened chamber." Design your own darkened chamber using the instructions given on pages 19-21 in the book *Understanding Photography* by George Sullivan.

Inventory all the different types of film which are sold. Survey everyone at your school and local community to discover which type more people like and report the results to the class.

Imagine that your camera is a creature from another planet. Write a story about how you keep this little alien off your neck and out of your eyes.

In a comparison chart, contrast the box camera, Polaroid camera, 35mm Rangefinder, Twin-Lens Reflex, Single-Lens Reflex, Ultraminiature camera and View camera.

Write a brief explanation for each of these types of lenses: standard, workhorse, wide-angle and telephoto.

Numerous accessories are available to the shutterbugs. Decide on the necessity of each of the following for your class: lens shade, exposure meter, filters and tripod.

Imagine you were in charge of a photgraphy studio, what would you do first?

Take pictures of small things up close—like a ladybug; high up—like an airplane; moving things—like an animal.

Click pictures at unusual angles—through wavy glass; of people in action and with special effects.

Take candid shots of your family and compose a photo essay.

For really abstract photographs, try taking pictures of people reflected in car bumpers, things reflected in water and things seen in the moonlight.

In creating photos, several things are important to keep in mind: center of interest, arrangement and balance, depth, directional lines and cropping. Define each of these.

Find the Words

IT'S PHOTOGRAPHY

Take the words *It's Photography* and make as many smaller words as you can out of the letters. You can only use each letter as many times as it appears in *It's Photography.*

Example: graph

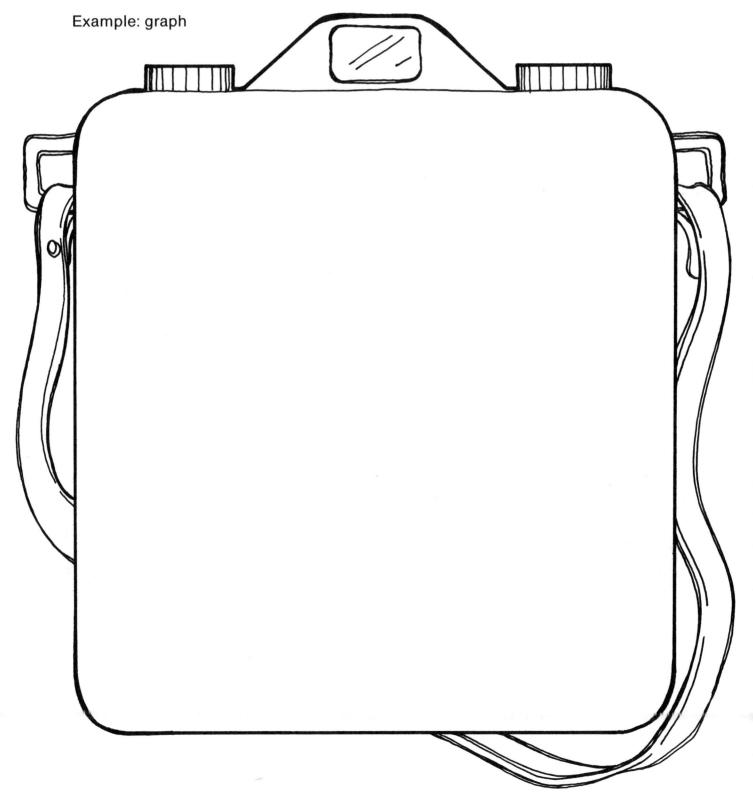

GA1321

Photography

```
              P F S F W
          L I E Z L C D M F H I G E
        Z G T D O R M O U K R X B I N F G
        B N G X L Z V W L W J W F R Q R K D B
        S K X L K S O T R H F J P F Z X D N G V X
        K C Y C K G L M T K X S N Q Z K N D R E N Q F
       F I L T E R S O C G J D I X L R M I P V K Y L P N
      W N V S R V L F V S R K F Z E T F O X D J F A I Q R J
      Z G N B U Q T B Q T J L N X D I J P V J P S D N F O C T Z
      L P H R T Z C U N F W S N G X I L U E O I X V D K V A U J
      V B N S V O A S P I H L F B L T Q V N R H K F A V W K G T W S
     B E H V Y S M J I K J R T D S A Q Y N P E H N O J O J S I V M C R
     F D G J L G N U V K Z O J C F J W H R D X L D K M K J S R J S U T
    G Q T S G Q L C U Z L Z N P I N V W K N W P X H M F A U D G F N V D I
    W D I B X F N K V O J O X F G T S L I J N O R O P H O T O G R A P H Q
   N Q S B L Z S G R T N I C A M E R A V F H P S D F R S J X O U V X W H F V
   X Z H N B D W V S C B Z G H V D F S J T Y Z E K S Q F G W T N B P J A H S
   D V Y S G M C M R L J W V R W C T J F F K L D S N J V J V N D Z V M D K I
  K O J Z V W N D S B I Z D P V Z L J S I H C G J H T L C F T F E O A N Z C H J
  F G C G N M Z X C F C W C W Q W F C X L K D B Z U S R U N O Q R S V Q S E G T
  H V C D Q M E F T I K Y B J H T F R I M Y G M R T S M V F J R E M D B J V B K
  O J D R F Z E N J P I G V G V O U F G F H B O E T T V S T Z B X Z W C L N I Z
  F T N W S A S N Z N N Z H F S O H K C U T O J E I J H K I T P K Z M C N H
  N E G A T I V E D G S C V S Z D K V F S O N J R L W J D N T O S D Z C N P
  Z C N H C F Y P E H S R V P N T G R G C O X B J C F T U R F S D B H N S L
  J X L E N S E S N X C H F N I K T D V B P S J S O J M A U E F B H F V
  B N G I N F T W J R Q D P B M I S V H N W S T V K G D F N D K H L C J
  V S W E K N U D T X S G L B X J H F M F H J M S C G X G H D T C F
  Q H M C I W I D E A N G L E J W P R S K R C N J L D V W T Q N J W
  M W T R I P O D O J B Z A Z V K E D C X B E H V B U F N T J S
   T E Z F I S C O H N F D F Z A N G L E S J U G Z A O U T D
   F B J K F O A T F L M N X Y A G Z R P L T I W Q S Z N F N
   F K F X D P R F P Z O V T V S L K E T H F B T V E A B
   N D E V E L O P I N G R D F J K X V X V H Q M C N
    Z C K X W G D N K J K Z W Z L F U C D J D O C
    O P N F C I O H T C J L H B W J D Q Y T G
     J T Z F W F B K Y F N Z M O U H Z I X
      N Y L G P B W V D F J F E T D S O
       N G R C V J P Z U A H N F
          J O C A G
```

The following words can be found hidden across and down in the puzzle above.

UNDEREXPOSED	TRIPOD	SHUTTER
PHOTOGRAPH	LENSES	ANGLES
WIDE-ANGLE	OVEREXPOSED	CAMERA
NEGATIVE	DEVELOPING	FILM
FILTERS	CLICKING	

14

The World's Greatest Photographer

You are the world's greatest photographer, and as such, you are looking for new and unusual shots to shoot with your camera. Name at least ten different things that you can think of which are really "special" and of which you might want camera shots. Make a list below.

GA1321

Pirates, Buccaneers and Privateers Week

Teacher Tactics

Setting the Stage: Pose these statements to your class: "Have you ever read a book about pirates or seen a movie about them? We're going to discuss pirates this week, and you may learn some things you haven't heard before. Pay attention and I guarantee you'll become a little closer to pirates."

With the class, create three-sided pirate hats using tagboard.

A possible vocabulary list you could go over with the class might include such terms as:

barnacle—hard-shelled sea animal
tricorne—a three-cornered hat
cutlasses—short, heavy curved swords
booty—stolen goods
ransom letters—to symbolize captivity
port—left side of a ship
captives—prisoners
provisions—food and water
cargo—freight
bandolier—bright cloth sash
fleet—a group of ships
mast—a vertical pole rising from the deck
cannons—artillery/guns

Some of the more commonly heard quotes might have included:
"Aye, aye, sir," said the mate.
"Man the pumps!"
"Batten the hatches!"
"Ride out the storm!"
"Hoist the flag!"
"Sail off the starboard bow!"
"Prepare for boarding!"
"Walk the plank!"

If possible, ask an expert in piracy to come in and speak to the class. Allow time for a question and answer session.

GA1321

Pirates, Buccaneers and Privateers Week

Absolutely Adaptable Activities

Many pirates changed their real names to nicknames, for instance Edward Teach became Blackbeard and Calico Jack, Timberhead, Black Bart, Red Hand and Barbarossa also changed their names. Choose ten modern pirates from the news and give them new names based on what they've done.

If you could make three changes in a pirate, what would they be?

In pirate terms, the highest in command was the pirate captain, next was the quartermaster and finally came the crew. What is the chain of command on a ship in the United States Navy?

What if there had never been such things as pirates? How would the world be different? What things would stay the same?

You are a TV news reporter. Describe the scene you'd see aboard a pirate ship.

Some of the most famous pirates were Blackbeard, Bartholomew Roberts, Samuel Bellamy, Anne Bonny, Mary Read, Henry Morgan, L'Olonnois, Calico Jack, Timberhead, Black Bart, Red Hand, Barbarossa and Captain Kidd. Research one or more of these famous buccaneers and try to discover the "why" behind what each accomplished.

There were many different kinds of pirate ships—Egyptian punt ships, Roman merchant ships, Phoenician galleys, Egyptian sailing ships, Roman galleys, Roman coasters and Judean merchant ships, just to name a few. Look up some of these ships in a pirate topic book like *Pirates and Privateers,* by Jeremy Pascall. Then design your very own pirate ship on a large piece of drawing paper and make it as detailed as possible.

Imagine you are in charge of a pirate ship. What would you do first?

Pirates were also called sea rovers, pickaroons, ladrones, freebooters, filibusters, corsairs and buccaneers. Make a list of all the names teenagers and younger kids have been called over the past ten years like nerd, Mr. Potatohead, etc.

Privateers were commissioned by the government to capture enemy ships, and unlike pirates, gave half their treasures back to the king. Who in the modern day world would we classify as a privateer?

Create a commemorative stamp displaying either a famous pirate, a famous pirate vessel or a Jolly Roger pirate flag.

You are living in the days of the pirates and want to rebel but are afraid of losing your life. Write an editorial to the newspaper, sharing your ideas with him for a "pirate wipeout."

Today, air pirates hijack airplanes, and sea pirates use powerboats to ship illegal goods. It just goes to show you some pirates never die? Design a game comparing the old with the new—past day pirates with modern day ones. Use a file folder as your gameboard.

Write a description of a treasure that you might like to discover.

GA1321

"Aye, Aye, Jolly Roger"

The pirates' Jolly Roger was a flag with the emblem of the pirates' ships displayed on it. Most featured a skull and crossbones or had to do in some way with death.

Your job is to create a modern day Jolly Roger for the modern day pirate, one who loves life and wants to help save lives, not destroy. In the space below, draw this modern pirate flag, making it as detailed as possible.

GA1321

Buried Treasure

Few pirates ever buried their treasures as was once commonly believed; rather they quickly spent their stolen or newfound riches as fast as they could. Therefore, few treasure maps were ever made.

Your job is to originate one of the few maps which *was* made by drawing very specific directions and imagining a place where "treasure" *could* be buried. Use your classroom, school or neighborhood as the area for the burial place. Make the map look old by wiping light-colored coffee or tea on it after you've completed it. Lightly tear around the edges. Exchange with a classmate and see whether he can figure it out! Have fun!

North ∘∘∘ East ∘∘∘ South ∘∘∘ West

GA1321

Pirates vs. Privateers

Privateers were commissioned by their government to capture enemy pirate ships and relieve them of their treasures, keeping half for themselves and returning the other half to their royalty.

Crews of merciless pirates roamed the seas attacking any treasure-filled merchant ship they might stumble upon. Since they were so skilled and had been at sea so long, they had little difficulty acquiring the riches they sought.

Imagine you are a privateer in search of the great pirate Blackbeard and his crew. Write about your many escapades in and out of the sea and how you finally capture the "Old Devil."

GA1321

You're a Real Gem Week

Teacher's Tactics

Setting the Stage: Pose this to your class: "Does anyone in here have a rock collection? Did you know that rocks are in a larger category called minerals, and also included in this category are gems? We'll be discussing gems, rocks and minerals this week, and hopefully you'll learn more about them."

"Coal is the fuel which made the Industrial Revolution possible."—Anonymous
If you are studying the Industrial Revolution, see how this quote fits in.

The earth's crust contains almost 3000 different known substances called minerals. Brainstorm with your class a list of as many different kinds of minerals as you can.

Most libraries contain a mineral collection which you can check out and utilize with your class. If the minerals aren't already numbered, number each and see how many your class can learn over the course of a week. Also, use a microscope to show students a different view of minerals they hadn't seen in the past. You'd be surprised how many of your students have mineral collections of their own.

What is the difference between a gem and a rock? What about a mineral and a stone? Answer these questions and more in a forum you present for the class.

Gem cutting is a very special profession, as over the years, gem cutters have studied the very best ways to cut stones. If there is a gem cutter in your area, invite him to come and share with the class his profession and perhaps give a demonstration of gem cutting.

If you have the funding, order your very own class a set of minerals from a scientific supply house.

Create a class bulletin board display of minerals, rocks and gems. Assign every person in the room a different job and set it up over the course of one afternoon or one week. Vary the board between magazine pictures, handmade pictures and information cards.

Take your class to a gem and mineral show that may visit your town sometime during the year.

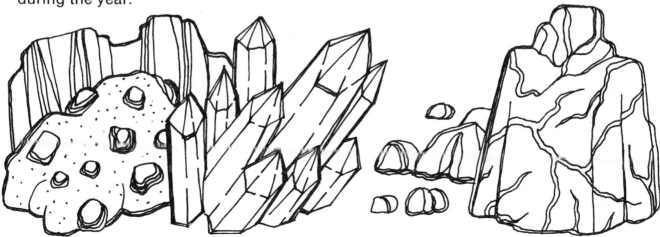

You're a Real Gem Week

Absolutely Adaptable Activities

Illustrate each of the following in a Rock and Roll booklet: granite, feldspar, quartz, mica, limestone, marble, hematite, pyrite, sphalerite, garnet, topaz, zircon, emerald, sapphire, ruby, lapis lazuli and turquoise or illustrate on a poster, in an informational book or a watercolor collection.

Royalty has always had the finest gems in their crown jewels. Research the British Crown Jewels to determine exactly what is in their collection.

Why do you think adults are so fascinated with gems?

"You're a gem." "Rock and roll." Name as many different sayings as you can think of that have to do with minerals, rocks, gems, etc.

Pearls form on the insides of oysters. Find all you can about oyster diving, the process of how a pearl is made, and then make a list of all the things which are made from pearl.

If you were a gem, what would you be? Why?

Mining is a very important industry which takes minerals out of the ground. There are several different kinds of mining. Research one of the types of mining and write an informational poem.

In an "All About Rocks and Minerals" booklet, define the following: *double refraction, compound, composition, hardness, cavities, geodes, twinned crystal, cleavage, heat proof, transparent, fool's gold, smelting, pig iron, refined, native elements, gold leaf, nuggets, gold bars, hallmark* and *opaque.*

Back in the days of the Gold Rush, "panning" was done in rivers and streams and other bodies of water. Give a demonstration for the class, showing them "how it's done!"

Do all gems and minerals look alike? What makes them different?

In a chart compare and contrast metallic minerals and nonmetallic minerals.

Without using a dictionary, brainstorm all the words you can think of that begin with *min-.*

If you could dream of being the richest person in the world, which gems would you dream of owning?

Compose a play about the "Rock That Took over the World."

Invent a comic strip where the greatest gem ever seen has been stolen from the richest woman in the world.

GA1321

Mix 'Em Up

Try to see if you can decipher the following mixed-up words into their real forms. Draw a line to connect the correct mixed word to the real word.

1. E T O N M S I E L   FELDSPAR

2. U R A Z Q T   EMERALD

3. R F P L D E S A   TOPAZ

4. E N T R G I A   TURQUOISE

5. Z O P T A   PYRITE

6. L E A M R E D   MARBLE

7. I C M A   LIMESTONE

8. T P I E Y R   GRANITE

9. U Q I R U O E S T   MICA

10. M R B E A L   QUARTZ

23

GA1321

A Gem of a Story Problem

A long time ago there lived a miser named Mica. He mined minerals like granite, feldspar, quartz, limestone, marble, hematite, pyrite, garnet, topaz, zircon, emerald, sapphire, ruby and turquoise.

1. On one day alone he mined 24 pounds (10.8 kg) of granite, 42 pounds (18.9 kg) of feldspar and 12 pounds (5.4 kg) of limestone.

2. The next day he went out and he mined 29 pounds (13.05 kg) of quartz, 15 pounds (6.75 kg) of marble and 33 pounds (14.85 kg) of hematite.

3. On the third day Mica mined 11 pounds (4.95 kg) of pyrite, 8 pounds (3.6 kg) of topaz, 5 pounds (2.25 kg) of garnet and 39 pounds (17.55 kg) of zircon.

4. On the fourth day he mined 43 pounds (19.35 kg) of emerald, 15 pounds (6.75 kg) of sapphire, 27 pounds (12.15 kg) of ruby and 22 pounds (9.9 kg) of turquoise.

Your job is to find out how many total pounds (kilograms) of minerals Mica mined each day. On which day did he mine the most? How many total pounds (kilograms) of minerals did Mica mine in four days? Good luck!

(For a really big challenge, find the average number of pounds [kilograms] of minerals that Mica mined each day.)

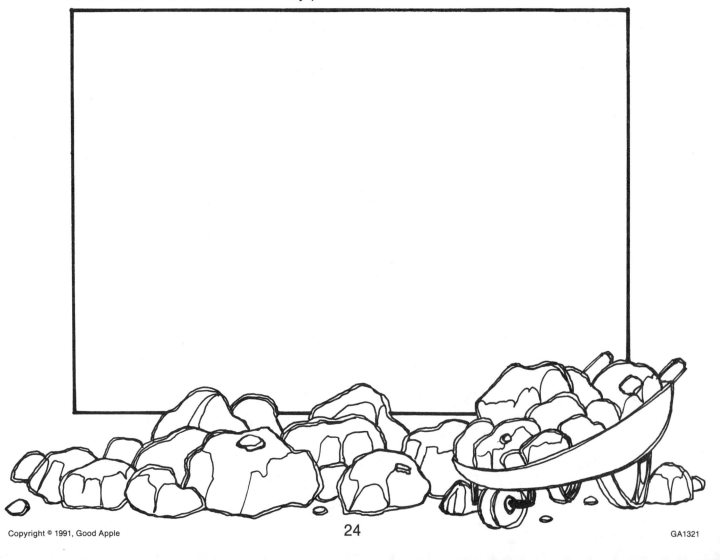

GA1321

Draw Your Wildest Mineral!

Use your wildest imagination to draw:

1. a piece of turquoise with handles

2. a gem with a bow tie

3. a pearl with six arms

4. a piece of topaz with an accordion

5. a semi-invisible piece of sphalerite

6. an 80-pound (36 kg) piece of gold

7. a battery-operated piece of marble

8. mica with five balloons attached to it

9. a piece of zircon with a giant hook out the top

10. an emerald with wheels

11. a multicolored ruby ring

12. feldspar in an open box

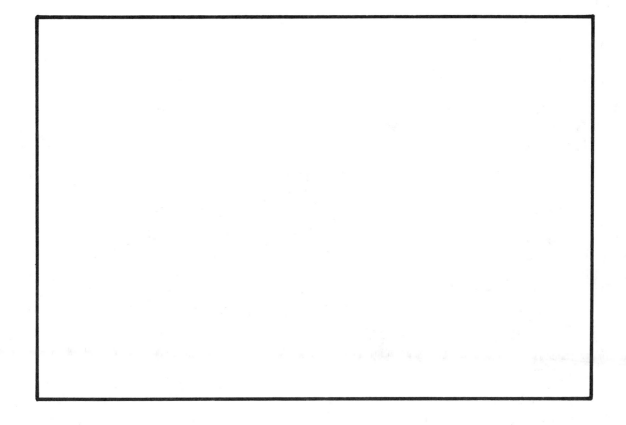

GA1321

Playful Pet Week

Teacher Tactics

Setting the Stage: Pose this to your class: "Does anyone in here have a pet or more than one pet at home? Let's hear what some of your pets are. This week we will be discussing pets, some common and some a little more exotic. Be prepared to learn more about pets."

The American Humane Association offers a complete Humane Educational classroom kit (HE-700) with posters, bookmarks and teaching suggestions for $1.50. A rental film list (HE-7500) at no cost and selected films on animals (HE-751) for $1.25 are also available from:

American Humane Association
P.O. Box 1266
Denver, CO 80201

Please add 20 percent of net for shipping costs (25-cent minimum).

Visit a pet store with your class. If time permits, ask the store owner to explain some of the more exotic pets living there. Leave time for questions from the students. On your return to the classroom, ask students to write lists of what they learned and make it a contest to see who learned the most.

Ask a pet shop owner to visit your classroom and possibly bring some of the animals from his store. Allow a question and answer time for the students. Finally, after he has gone, ask students to write thank-you notes.

Write for:

"A Nutrition Guide for Pet Owners" (FDA 74-2021)
U.S. Government Printing Office
Supt. of Documents
Washington, D.C. 20402

Write a letter to "Thank You for Helping Us" and "Fitting 'Em in . . ." (chart) to:

Bureau of Land Management
U.S. Dept. of Interior
Washington, D.C. 20240

GA1321

Playful Pet Week

Absolutely Adaptable Activities

What does a cat become after it is six months old? (Seven months old!) This is a riddle. Write three pet riddles of your own.

Write a story about a dog that turned into a cat.

All reptiles, snakes, turtles and lizards are absolutely silent. In other words, they make absolutely no noise. Name as many things living and nonliving as you can think of that are also silent.

Scientists and pet owners alike have found the terms *reptiles* and *amphibians* a bit clumsy when said together time after time. Instead, reptiles and amphibians are called *herps* meaning "crawling things." Name everything that crawls. How many could be called pets?

Write a letter to your local Humane Society telling how you feel about the treatment of their animals.

High temperatures will speed up a snake, while low temperatures will do exactly the opposite. Make two columns on your paper, one labeled *cool/cold* and one labeled *warm/hot*. Now list under each heading all the pets that feel more comfortable in that temperature.

All gecko lizards make good pets with the exception of the Tokay gecko, the largest of the geckos. In fact, in one pet store a sign reads "TOKAY GECKOS—You Catch 'Em—$10.00, We Catch 'Em—$20.00. Research the gecko and design the perfect habitat in which you could keep one.

The turtle is an omnivore, while most other reptiles are carnivores. No reptile is a herbivore. What do these terms mean? Look them up in a dictionary and write a short meaning for each.

Different kinds of parrots like to engage in different kinds of activity—displays of affection, talking, acrobats, hanging, swinging, rolling around, being tricky, clearing their throats and blowing their noses. Choose any other kind of pet and list all the kinds of activities it engages in.

Imagine that a butterfly flew into a pet store and turned into one of the animals. Which one would it be?

Hermit crabs, fiddler crabs, gerbils and chameleons all will make wonderful pets, as long as you have the right home, water, food, possibly other animals of the same type, heat if needed, etc. Make a list for each of the above animals which will answer each of these categories.

Would you describe a dog as friendly and outgoing and a cat as standoffish and cool? Why do you think they act that way? Write a funny story about a happy and friendly dog and a really snobbish cat.

See if you can find out the smallest and the biggest kinds of dogs.

A cat on your block is stuck in a tree. Give at least ten ways you can get it down.

Having a fish that you can watch is supposed to make you feel better. Write a short paper about all the animals that have the power to make you feel better.

GA1321

Troubles with Pets

Polly has a parrot with a sore throat. Igor has an iguana with spots. Barry has a bunny with fur that is falling out. And Sally has a snake with slippery skin. Each one of the four kids has been having some troubles with his/her pet, and needs some suggestions.

Write to each of the four children and tell each what to do about his/her pet problem.

GA1321

Pet Math Match

IGUANA
10 – 4 =

CHAMELEON
2 + 5 =

HAMSTER
2 + 8 =

FISH
8 – 5 =

BUNNY
1 + 7 =

29

GA1321

Beyond Belief!

A new animal was on display at the pet store. The animal was part bird, part lizard and part snake.

In the space below, draw what you think this new animal looked like.

National Newspaper Week

(Begins First or Second Sunday in October)

Teacher Tactics

Setting the Stage: Pose the following to your class: "Do any of you read a daily newspaper? If so, which sections do you read? Let's make a list on the board. This week we'll be studying the newspaper and each of its sections."

Two activity sheets (with twenty-one activities) which use newspaper comics, cartoons and visuals are offered free from the *Hartford Courant*, 285 Broad Street, Hartford, CT 06115.

Visit a newspaper with your class and take a guided tour. When you get back to the classroom, discuss each section that you saw. Have the students make lists of things they learned about newspapers.

Invite a newspaper reporter to the classroom and interview him/her. Prepare the interview questions prior to the visit. Assign different members of the class to ask the questions. After the reporter has left, review the answers given.

Create a class newspaper wherein class members write autobiographies; biographies of teachers and principals; stories; comic strips; interviews of staff and students; opinion polls; happenings around school and extra ideas about holidays, special events, etc.

GA1321

National Newspaper Week

Absolutely Adaptable Activities

This ad was seen in the classification ads of a newspaper:
FERRARI 246 DINO Coupe, 18 K ml, xlnt condition, Pts & X tires
Documentation and records, $125,000 OBO, Call Steve Lewis.
What do you think *K, ml, xlnt, Pts, X* and *OBO* mean?

The Sports section of the newspaper usually puts out stories about many different sports. Brainstorm a list of the different sports which might be discussed in a newspaper.

Car dealers like to buy full-page ads in newspapers. What might be all the things they'd include in a full-page ad?

Design an invitation for a party at the newspaper office.

Sometimes, in the Editorial section of the newspaper, letters to the editor exist. These are letters which express people's opinions and how they feel about specific topics. Write a letter to your editor, sharing your ideas about a topic that really concerns you.

The front page of the newspaper lists some of the other stories that you'll find in other parts of the paper, as well as the most important stories of the day. Write a front-page story yourself about what you feel is the biggest story of the day. Make sure to answer the Who? What? Where? Why? When? and How? questions.

What kinds of jobs would you find at the newspaper office? Make a list.

Take any headline and write a story to go with it.

One section of the newspaper discusses issues that happen close to home—in your city and in your state. Call the newspaper's city desk, tell them you are a student, and find out one of the top city stories for the day. Then write your own version of the story.

Many newspapers have an Entertainment section, which gives movie reviews, movies currently showing, celebrity stories and a listing of TV shows. Write a review of one of your favorite TV shows. Give it a "thumbs up" or "thumbs down" and list your reasons.

Create a comic strip about Benny the Bear and his sidekick Hobo Joe.

What do you think the editor, the man who receives all the mail and edits the paper, thinks about all that mail that comes to him?

GA1321

Who's New in the News?

Many people are in the news, some more than others. Pick up a copy of today's newspaper and find some of the names that are presented the most.

Choose one name and read as much about that individual as possible. Ask your teacher if there are any other references you can use to find out more about this person. Then write a one-page essay in the space below about the person.

GA1321

Comic Strip Mania

Create a comic strip which features a funny-looking dog named Barney and his best pal Sparky, the talking parrot. The basic story is that Barney and Sparky are afraid of going into the alley, because Bruno, a Doberman pinscher, keeps scaring them off. What do they do? Remember, comic strips have to be either witty or funny or both.

Newspaper Notes

The Sunday newspaper is virtually filled with many different sections and even has different parts to each section.

Below you are to list all the parts and sections to the newspaper on Sunday. Good luck!

1.
2.
3.
4.
5.
6.
7.
8.
9.
10.
11.
12.
13.
14.
15.
16.
17.
18.
19.
20.

GA1321

Fire Prevention Week

Teacher Tactics

Setting the Stage: Pose the following to your class: "Have you ever thought about what you'd do if your house was on fire? Well, this is Fire Prevention Week, and in honor of that title, we're going to all know what we'd do in the event of a fire by the end of the week."

For more information about Fire Prevention, write:
National Fire Protection Association
470 Atlantic Ave.
Boston, MA 02210

Fire Prevention Week is always held during the week of October 8th, which just happens to be the anniversary of the Great Chicago Fire in 1871. It began when Mrs. O'Leary's cow supposedly kicked over a lantern in the barn at 137 De Koven Street in downtown Chicago. The fire rampaged over 21,000 acres (8400 ha), burned 17,000 buildings, killed an unknown number of people and left close to 100,000 homeless.

Invite a fire fighter to the classroom to discuss fire safety and all the ways a fire can start. Hold a question and answer session after his speech.

Visit a fire station and receive the grand tour—you may see paramedic vehicles, fire engines, fire-fighting equipment, fire fighters, and of course, the fire station.

GA1321

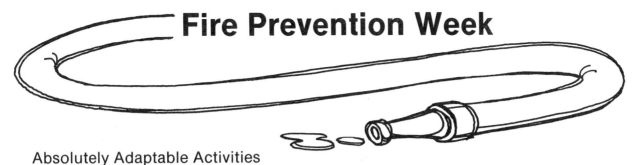

Fire Prevention Week

Absolutely Adaptable Activities

The fire engine is a very complex machine with all of its hoses, water, ladders, rescue equipment, pump, siren, light and foam unit. Draw a fire truck and label all its parts.

Fire drills are for the purpose of guiding you to where you'll go if there is a fire. In your own house, plan a fire drill and then actually hold one.

Oil and chemical fires cannot be put out with water, or they will spread. Try to discover with what these types of fires should be doused.

Forest fires cannot be put out with water because they're too big. Try to think of some other ways to stop forest fires, and then look up the answer in a book about forest fires.

Preventing a fire is like _____.

What is the importance of the fire bell? What would happen if a station lost its bell?

Describe the clothing and equipment that fire fighters use when fighting a fire. How fast do fire fighters dress for a fire?

What is traffic supposed to do while the fire truck is coming down the road?

Write an article about fire prevention for your school newspaper.

What are all the different ways to leave a burning building that you can think of?

Why are hot ashes from your fireplace so dangerous? What should be done with them?

What are all the parts to a fire fighter's outfit? Name them.

Describe an ordinary day in the life of a fire fighter (without a fire).

Write a paragraph that explains to younger students why false alarms are so terrible.

Name some helpful hints for fire prevention.

Write a letter to your local fire fighters and tell them how you feel about the job they're doing.

Name all the ways flashlights can help out in a fire.

Explain how smoke detectors work and how they should be used in your home.

Name two kinds of apparatus that fire fighters can place on the ground onto which victims of a building fire can jump.

Make believe you wake up in the middle of the night and you smell smoke! Make a list of what you would do.

                                       GA1321

Fire Fighter Stamp

Create a Fire Fighter Commemorative Stamp which really shows what fire fighting is all about.

GA1321

Stuck with No Where to Go!

You are stuck in a burning building and no help is in sight. Write a story telling about how you get out of this building you're in, using every means of escape you have.

GA1321

Promoting Fire Fighters

Create a billboard advertisement promoting the fire fighters in your town. Design a catchy phrase and a bold picture.

Poetry Week

Teacher Tactics

Setting the Stage: Pose this to your class: "How many of you like to rhyme? Where in life can we rhyme? That's right! In poetry! This week we will look at many different kinds of poetry and write quite a few kinds of poetry ourselves. Let's have fun!"

Some poets for students to research might be Henry Wadsworth Longfellow, Robert Frost and Edgar Allen Poe.

If you want to read to your students, two poets whom they will enjoy are Shel Silverstein and Jack Prelutsky. They're wonderful!

Create a class mobile of individual student's poetry using sticks, fishing line and index cards. The poem could be written on one side of the card while a picture illustrating the poem could be on the other side.

Build a unique learning center on poetry. Cut a "tree" out of a large box. Paint it to look like a tree, and write POET-TREE on the top of it. Then on leaf-shaped cards write poetry tasks. You can have different colors of green at the top for the "tree" for specific activities, while colored leaves at the bottom of the "tree" might tell students how to do the various types of poetry. The leaf-shaped cards can be hung on the "TREE" with curtain hooks.

Invite a local poet to the classroom to share his/her poems with the class. Be sure to ask the poet to explain the meaning of the poetry.

Explain to the class the definitions for the following types of poetry: name, animal, ABC, tanka, limerick, haiku, holiday, quatrain, diamante, rainbow, cinquain and concrete poetry.

GA1321

Poetry Week

Absolutely Adaptable Activities

Create a name poem about yourself and one about a friend.

Write an animal poem about a small goat and its mama.

Design an ABC poem about the fifty states and what happens in many of them.

Research and write a paper about the poet Carl Sandburg, and share it with the class.

Create a poem in the tanka form about a desert animal.

Write a limerick about two or three of your friends or famous people.

Rhyme with *BAT* every word you can think of.

Design a poem in the haiku form about autumn.

Research and write a paper about the poet Robert Browning and share it with the class.

Choose a holiday. Write a holiday poem about it.

Create a humorous quatrain using the *abab* pattern.

Write a poem using the diamante form.

Choose five colors and write a rainbow poem and illustrate it.

Take the words *hum, ham* and *him* and rhyme each one as many times as possible.

Research and write a composition on the poet William Shakespeare. Share one or part of one of his poems with the class.

Research either Emily Dickinson or William Wordsworth and share what you've found with the class.

Using the cinquain form, write a poem about monkeys.

Write a concrete poem within its shape.

Write a brief biography of the poet Walt Whitman. Include his achievements. Share a poem of Walt Whitman's with the class.

GA1321

Concrete—It's Sweet!

Concrete poetry means writing a few verses about a specific item or idea and then placing those verses into the shape of the item.

For example:

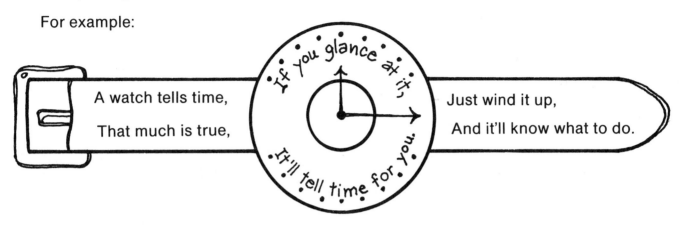

A watch tells time,

That much is true,

If you glance at it,

It'll tell time for you.

Just wind it up,

And it'll know what to do.

Now, you write your own concrete poem!

GA1321

ABC—It's as Easy as 1-2-3

An ABC poem is done by writing out the entire alphabet, taking a topic, and writing one word for every letter which describes that topic. For example, if the topic was "students," you could write:

Aware
Bright
Caring
Daring
Excellent
Fun
Great
Happy
Interesting
Jovial
Kind
Loving
Moving
Nice
Optimistic
Pleasant
Quick
Real
Sincere
Tender
Understanding
Versatile
Wise
eXtraordinary
Young
Zany

Now, write your own ABC poem about pets:

A
B
C
D
E
F
G
H
I
J
K
L
M

N
O
P
Q
R
S
T
U
V
W
X
Y
Z

44

GA1321

Free Verse—No Rehearse

Free verse poetry has no rhyme. It's just a collection of lines that all relate to the same topic. Here's an example.

The moon was rising high,
While the animals played freely.
A dark shadow filled the earth,
And the night had just begun.

Now you try a free verse poem four to eight lines long.

GA1321

Creepy Creatures Week

Teacher Tactics

Setting the Stage: Think back to a scary movie you've seen or a scary book you've read. Were there any scary creatures in either of them? Well, this week we're going to hear about a creepy assortment of creatures and their antics.

A senile scientist spends hours in his laboratory creating scientific blunders. This time he's really gone mad and the result is Frankenstein! Brainstorm with your class at least five cures for this blunder.

King Kong has a problem. He has nothing to wear to the monster's ball. Ask the class to brainstorm what he might wear.

For four weeks, monsters have plagued your community. Everyone is pretty well fed up with practical jokes, so they need some suggestions as to what to do. Pose this problem to your class and try to come up with a few answers.

This unit lends itself perfectly to the week of Halloween. Try to incorporate the activities until your Halloween party arrives.

GA1321

Creepy Creatures Week

Absolutely Adaptable Activities

Write the "Legend of the Ghoulish Phantom" and his escape from the coffin.

Who is the Abominable Snowman and why have stories been passed down from generation to generation? Research this creature and report back to the class.

Write about the time when you met a creepy creature and all that you did together.

Dracula has decided to wed Greta the Ghost. Design a wedding announcement for the two.

You are in a boat on a Scottish Lake when all of a sudden, in front of your eyes, stands the Loch Ness Monster! Write diary entries for what happens next.

Invent a recipe for a gigantic creepy creature and its sidekick Winnie.

Brainstorm a list of all the scary creatures you've seen or read about in the past. Create monster stew on paper in a big stew pot. Dump all those monsters in.

It's nighttime and you're out for a moonlit ride. You hear someone behind you and when you turn around, who is sitting atop his horse but the Headless Horseman! Compose a song to portray how you feel.

There's been a breakout from the hospital down the street and Cyclops is on the loose! You are all alone in your house when suddenly you hear a rattling sound at the window in the den! List five different things you could do in this situation.

Name some places where King Kong would feel at home.

Your family is traveling down the road when all of a sudden, a huge, furry creature hits the car. When you get out, you realize there's a good chance it's Big Foot. You don't know if he's dead or alive, so you . . . . Create your own ending to this story starter.

Aliens have settled down in your state, and there are twelve different kinds. Design a calendar which illustrates all twelve.

An evil sorcerer gazes into his crystal ball. Give five predictions of what he might see.

Write a TV news story about the day the creepy creatures came to town.

A sea serpent slithered out of the water and went straight for the video arcade and proceeded to clear out the place. Name all the things that could be done to remove the sea serpent without hurting the slithering creature.

47

GA1321

King Kong Visits

King Kong is a huge, hairy creature who banged his chest and scared the townspeople. The town now needs some suggestions about how to take care of removing King Kong from the city limits, without any violence occurring.

Make a list below that describes different ways to remove King Kong from the town with the least amount of chaos, violence and inhumanity.

48

GA1321

Monsters' Yard Sale

A yard sale took place in January 1900. The Abominable Snowman earned $90.00. Big Foot earned $50.00 at the sale. A visiting sea serpent earned $30.00.

Cyclops pulled in $80.00 because he sold a lawn mower. The Headless Horseman made a measly $10.00 because his head wasn't really in it. King Kong stretched $20.00 out of some visiting monkeys.

The Loch Ness Monster netted $70.00 at the yard sale. Frankenstein showed up and earned $40.00 for his goods. A wandering ghost sold $60.00 worth of wares while she was there.

The question is, how much total money was made at this yard sale?

GA1321

Monster Scramble

Draw a line from the scrambled word to the correct spelling.

1. COCSLPY   BIG FOOT

2. CLESONSH   ABOMINABLE SNOWMAN

3. OBFITOG   HEADLESS HORSEMAN

4. MBAALOENSMNIONAWB   FRANKENSTEIN

5. ASDHELOSEHSREMNA   CYCLOPS

6. SENPERASET   KING KONG

7. KGNIONKG   LOCH NESS

8. NNFKREANSEIT   SEA SERPENT

GA1321

Bicycles—The Spokes on You Week

Teacher Tactics

Setting the Stage: Pose the following to your class: "How many of you have ever ridden a bicycle? How many of you have ridden just short distances? How many of you like to go long distances? Bikes are fun, aren't they? This week we're going to be studying unicycles, bicycles, tricycles and tandems."

Call up a local bicycle shop that has been established. Inquire whether one of the owners might be interested in coming to your classroom and bringing a bike to explain all the parts. Then, if possible, engage in a question and answer session. Discuss what was said after the owner leaves.

Some vocabulary words you may want to define and/or research include *high-riser, sprocket, derailleur, coaster brake, caliper brakes, celerifere, pedicab, unicycle* and *tandem.*

Hold a Bicycle Appreciation Day and have all students who have bicycles bring them to school and spend some time letting each student "show off" his/her bicycle.

Invite a police officer to your classroom to discuss bicycle safety and the rules of the road.

GA1321

Bicycles—The Spokes on You Week

Absolutely Adaptable Activities

A bicycle handlebar is for _____. A bicycle spoke is for
_____.

Unicycles are traditionally used in circuses. Design circus acts that could be done with a bicycle and then a tricycle.

Conduct a survey throughout your neighborhood to determine how many there are of each of the following: unicycles, bicycles, tandems and tricycles.

Imagine you are an inventor and have invented the greatest bicycle machine ever. Write about it.

Compose a poetry book about some different experiences you've had while riding your bike.

Write a proposal to your City Council encouraging them to include more bicycle paths in your city.

You are a lonely bicycle. What can you do to make some friends?

There are unicycles, bicycles and tricycles. Design a pentacycle, a new kind of cycle with five wheels.

Write a TV commercial or jingle to advertise a new line of bicycle accessories. (Make up the "line" yourself!)

Create an adventure story about Barry and Bobby, the twin brothers who ride a bicycle built for two across the USA.

Design the fastest and best bicycle you can possibly imagine.

Bicycles have two wheels. Name all the other vehicles you can think of with wheels.

There are many different name brands for bicycles. Go to a bicycle store and jot down all the different brand names you can find.

Name all the different reasons people ride bicycles.

Draw a detailed diagram of a bicycle, labeling all the parts.

Make a poster of all the bicycle safety rules, complete with dos and don'ts.

Research the early bicycles of Comte Mede de Sivrac of France, Baron Karl von Drais of Germany, J. K. Starley of England and any others you can find.

Brainstorm all the words that begin with *bi-*.

You are going on a trip on your bicycle. Write about it when you return.

52

GA1321

Bicycle Math Marathon

One day at a bicycle marathon, 4 cyclists started at point A. They picked up 10 more at point B. At point C, 23 cyclists were waiting to join the pack.

On to point D, they collected 12 speedy cyclists. At point E, 17 individuals joined the pack. Then 2 poor souls dropped out due to dehydration. At point F, 29 more joined the troop. Finally, at point G, 3 stragglers entered the group.

How many total individuals participated in the bicycle marathon?

An Imaginary Trip

Write an imaginary letter to the International Youth Hostel Federation, which helps plan bicycle trips for young students and even shares inexpensive lodging throughout the United States.

You want to plan a bicycle tour. Get out your map and decide where you want to go and what you plan to do. Write your agenda to the Federation below.

54

GA1321

Focusing on the Bicycle

You are on the school newspaper staff. The article you are currently writing has to do with "the place the bicycle has in American society, especially with pre-teens." Write your article below, making sure it's as detailed as possible.

GA1321

The Wild, Wild West Week

Teacher Tactics

Setting the Stage: Pose this to your class: "How many of you like watching westerns on TV? The Wild, Wild West was a very exciting time and place to be. Cowboys and Indians, the Gold Rush and moving into the new frontier were just a few of the exciting things. We'll look at some of these items this week in our study of the Wild, Wild West.

Discuss with your students what it must have been like being the first people in a new territory, and how excited the new settlers must have felt. How did religion begin? Government? Law enforcement? What kinds of amusements were there? Land rights? Carry on a detailed discussion encompassing all of these areas.

The West brought many colorful characters. Some of these names you may want to assign for research: Jesse James, Billy the Kid, Wyatt Earp, "Wild Bill" Hickok, Buffalo Bill Cody, Calamity Jane, Sam Bass, Bat Masterson, Annie Oakley, Belle Starr, Daniel Boone, Kit Carson, William Clark, Sam Houston and William Lewis Sublette.

Some vocabulary words your class may need are *boot*—baggage compartment, *box*—coach driver's seat, *Charlie*—coach driver, *depot*—railroad station, *groom*—stableman, *leaders*—horses leading the team, *lines*—reins, *mustang*—wild horse, *repeater*—gun not needing reloading after each shot, *reinsman*—coach driver, *ribbons*—reins, *rig*—harness, *road agent*—highway robber, *wheel horses*—horses nearest the front of the coach, *whip*—coach driver.

Have your students write a story using the above vocabulary words.

GA1321

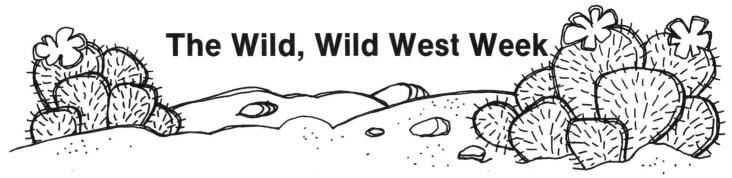

The Wild, Wild West Week

Absolutely Adaptable Activities

Do a make-believe interview with Jesse James. What would you ask?

The people of the Westward Movement were hardworking, courageous and seemed full of goodwill toward their neighbors. Do you know anyone who appears this same way today? Write a one-page essay about this person.

The first pioneers copied big "Palatine barns" from the Germans, and they even created a German weapon into what was called the Kentucky rifle. Circuit riders or preachers who wandered from place to place were donated by the Scotch-Irish. Look around your house and school and see if you can make a list of items that were contributed by other countries.

Pretend you live in the Wild, Wild West. What would you dress like? Draw a picture of yourself!

In 1775, Daniel Boone blazed the Wilderness Road through the Cumberland Gap, leading a group of settlers to make stake to their land. Imagine you were with Daniel Boone on this trip. What hardships might you have endured? Remember, no man had ever been there before.

Design a travel poster to the Wild, Wild West.

With all these settlers who came west, what problems do you see developing? What about government? What about land buying and selling? What about the Indians?

Do short reports on the Ordinance of 1785, the Northwest Ordinance and the Removal of the Indians.

In 1848, gold fever was everywhere! More than 100,000 Forty-Niners came quickly out to California where they could, if they chose to, stay in rooms which rented for $1000.00 a month and where eggs cost $10.00 each. Imagine how much those rooms and eggs would cost today!

There were many different stages and wagons when the West was settled. The 4-Seat Concord, 2-Seat Mud Wagon, Celebrity Wagon and Passenger Hack. Do a report on any one of these wagons.

Some of the guns of the time included the Philadelphia Derringer, Colt No. 3 Derringer, Sharps Four Barrel, Remington Derringer, English Perrerbox, 1815 Navy Colt and 10 Gauge Sawed-off Shotgun. Write a paper telling why you either are in favor of guns or not in favor of guns and give your reasons.

Who is your favorite Wild West character? Write a story about him/her and you in an interesting place.

GA1321

You Struck Gold!

Imagine that you lived in the Wild, Wild West in 1848, around the Gold Rush. You are poor, live in a small shack and you are looking for a dream—GOLD!

Well, you're out panning in the stream one day and guess what! You strike gold—BIG!

Write a story about how your life will change.

GA1321

Wild West Matchup

Match the term on the left with the definition on the right by drawing a line.

1. BOOT
2. DEPOT
3. GROOM
4. CHARLIE
5. RIG
6. JACKASS
7. MUSTANG
8. RIBBONS
9. TAPESTRY
10. BOX
11. WHIP
12. WHEEL HORSES
13. ROAD AGENT

a. COACH DRIVER
b. MALE DONKEY
c. REINS
d. WILD HORSE
e. BAGGAGE COMPARTMENT
f. RAILROAD STATION
g. COACH DRIVER
h. COACH DRIVER'S SEAT
i. STABLEMAN
j. HORSES NEAREST THE FRONT OF A COACH
k. HARNESS
l. HEAVY CLOTH
m. HIGHWAY ROBBER

GA1321

The James Gang's Problem

You have one problem to solve, and you must pay very close attention or you might miss something!

Jesse James was riding quickly after the holdup. He had just robbed the Cheyenne Bank with his brother Frank and their good friend Steven Bishop. They were planning on meeting just outside of town at their usual hangout, the Cave! Jesse had the money in his saddlebags, but he hadn't had time to count it yet.

As soon as Frank and Steven arrived, they all sat down to count the loot! Here is your problem:

The total number of dollars was $150.00. Now Steven's share was the smallest since he had just joined the gang. Frank's share was twice as much as Steven's since he was one of the brothers. Jesse's share was one-and-a-half times as much as Frank's because he was head honcho in the gang.

How much did each gang member get?

GA1321

Ringo Around the Flamingo Week

Teacher Tactics

Setting the Stage: Pose the following to your class: "Can you think of a bird with two stiltlike legs, a curved bill and stands 3 to 5 feet (.91 to 1.52 m) from the ground? You guessed it—a flamingo! This week we will be looking at the fascinating flamingo, and some interesting facts about it."

Go to the library and check out a videotape on flamingos. Ask students to take notes or upon the conclusion of the movie, ask students to write all they have learned.

Invite a zookeeper to the classroom to share his/her knowledge and expertise about flamingos. Hold a question and answer session afterwards. Write thank-you notes.

If your zoo has flamingos, take your class on a trip to the zoo. Have them study closely each of the flamingos for variations. Have students sketch a flamingo.

Wild flamingos once lived in Florida until all the poachers killed them for their beautiful feathers. Hold a class discussion about the rights and wrongs of poaching.

GA1321

Ringo Around the Flamingo Week

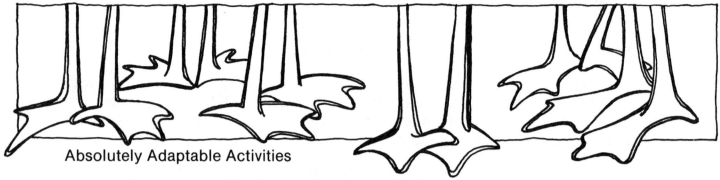

Absolutely Adaptable Activities

Imagine that you could talk to a flamingo. What kinds of things would you say?

Write and/or sing "The Ballad of the Flamingo."

Design an art gallery and include a variety of flamingos in different poses.

Flamingos live in colonies. Research and name at least three different animals that live in colonies too.

Design a bumper sticker, asking for more flamingos at your zoo.

Compose an article about a fashion show where ten of the twelve outfits were created out of flamingo feathers.

Write a tall tale about Fillamena Flamingo and her brood of fifty fancy but fitful five-month-old flamingos.

Interview the head flamingo. What questions will you ask?

Flamingos have webbed feet. List all the animals who could in any way be related to the word *web.*

Most zoologists classify flamingos into four groups—greater flamingos, lesser flamingos, Andean flamingos and James' flamingos. Brainstorm all the other things in life that come in four's.

Flamingos have long, sticklike legs for which they are most famous. Make a list of all the things for which animals (including humans) might use very long legs.

Choose any of the four types of flamingos and write an eight-line poem about it.

Imagine that you were a flamingo. What would three of your best wishes be?

Flamingos are beautiful creatures. Paint a picture of a group of them in a pond of water.

Create a cereal and box that revolve around the theme of flamingos.

Write a tongue twister about flamingos using the letter *f* as much as possible.

A group of flamingos have just moved into your neighborhood. Write a newspaper story about what it's like having a group of flamingos next door.

Create a story entitled "The Flamingos That Ruled the World."

62

Letter Brainstorm

FLAMINGOS

Take one of the letters in the word *flamingos* and brainstorm all the words that begin with that letter. (Example: F = first, finally, fact, fist, etc.)

63

Just Choose the Title

Choose one of the following titles and use it as a story starter.

FLAMINGOS JUST SAY NO!

A FONDLY REMEMBERED FLAMINGO FLIRTS WITH DEATH

FIFTY FLAMINGOS FIGHT FIRE

FLAMINGOS FLING FURRY FRIENDS AT FRITZ THE FELINE

GA1321

Flamingo Limericks

Write your own limerick. Here's an example of how one goes.

There once was a flamingo named Earl,	a
Who couldn't make friends with a girl.	a
Though he tried and tried,	b
He just cried and cried,	b
Because the girls wouldn't give him a whirl!	a

Now you try one.   Rhyme Scheme

A flamingo whose name was _____.	a
Really was a _____ concert fan.	a
He roamed from _____ to gig,	b
Even stopped to touch a _____,	b
And finally became a flamingo man!	a

Now see if you can write your very own flamingo limerick.

GA1321

National Stamp Collecting Week

(Second Week in November)

Teacher Tactics

Setting the Stage: Pose this to your class: "How many of you have noticed that sticky thing that goes in the corner of the envelope? Yes, the stamp! Well, are there any stamp collectors in here? This week we'll be studying stamps, stamp collecting and stamp designing. Let's get started!"

Buy a big bag of used stamps at a hobby store or toy store. Share them with your students and if the stamps are still attached to the envelopes, follow these few steps:

1. Cut as much of the paper around the stamp as possible.
2. Soak the stamps in a pan using warm tap water.
3. Wait two or three hours until the stamps separate from the paper.
4. Remove the stamps with tongs and then lay the stamps flat on some paper towels and place some heavy books on top of them.
5. Wait two to three hours until the stamps have dried.

Students should decide if they want to collect American or foreign, airmail, commemoratives or special delivery stamps. The post office sells "starter kits" for your students in case they are serious about stamp collecting. The post office also sells an informational book about stamps called *Stamps and Stories*.

Start a stamp club in your school. The United States Post Office promotes a club called the Benjamin Franklin Stamp Club, which is now in thousands of different schools across the country. Another possible club for your students is the Junior Philatelists of America. If you are a member, you can borrow records and films about stamps. To write to the club, send a self-addressed, stamped envelope to: Junior Philatelists of America, 1018 Foster Street, Evanston, Illinois 60201.

There are several types of stamps: *regular* or *definitive* stamps are found on most mail; *commemorative* stamps are issued to honor important events, persons or special subjects; *coil* stamps are issued in rolls; *airmail* stamps are used for sending mail overseas; *postage due* stamps are put on at the post office to show the postage paid was not enough. Share these different types of stamps with your class.

If any of your students would like to design a stamp, send their suggestions to: The Citizen's Stamp Advisory Commission, Stamp Development Branch, U.S. Postal Service, Washington, D.C. If students want a free Stamp Selection Booklet, write to U.S. Stamps Information Service, P.O. Box 23501, L'Enfant Plaza Station, Washington, D.C. A stock list of stamp issues and a booklet describing U.S. postage stamps and postal stationery is available by writing: Philatelic Sales Division, U.S. Postal Service, Washington, D.C. 20265. Please include a self-addressed, stamped envelope, 3¾" x 8¾" (9.52 x 22.22 cm) in size for any of the correspondence.

National Stamp Collecting Week

Absolutely Adaptable Activities

Design a bumper sticker that advertises National Stamp Collecting Week.

Create the most beautiful stamp you can possibly imagine. To make it actual size, use thin pencils and sharpened crayons.

Stamp collecting is the most popular hobby in the world. Name ten other hobbies that are also very popular.

Pretend you have the world's rarest stamp and it is worth one million dollars. How would you feel?

Some people think of stamps as windows on the world. If there was one place in the world you would like a window placed so you could look into it, what place would that be and why?

A large group of people enjoy stamp collecting because they feel that stamps are really works of art. Paint a picture that you feel, when minimized, would make a great stamp and a work of art.

Stamp collecting is _____. Being a stamp collector is _____.

Stamps can help with schoolwork. They can be used in class projects for science, history and geography. In addition, stamp collecting is a merit badge activity for Boy and Girl Scouts. Name at least ten other ways stamps can be used.

Postage stamps are good communicators. For instance, a single stamp, "Giving Blood Saves Lives," issued in 1971, was credited with acquiring enough blood donations for a six-month supply in American blood banks. What other kinds of messages can stamps give? Make a list.

In saving and preserving stamps, some special tools and materials are needed—an album to display your collection; tongs to move a stamp from one place to another; hinges for attaching stamps to the pages of your album; mounts; some plastic envelopes; a package of glassine envelopes to hold stamps until you're ready to put them into your album; stamp catalog to help you identify stamps and finally, a magnifying glass to help you see the details of stamps. Your job is to design an efficient and long-lasting kind of carry-all for all of this equipment.

Stamp collecting has quite a background. Research some of the outstanding moments in stamp collecting history and write a short report.

Create a "Stamp Glossary of Terms" where you define each of the following terms; *adhesive, block set of stamps, cancellation, coil, commemorative, condition, definitives, face value, first-day cover, gum, hinges, mint sheet, perforations, plate block, postmark, unused, used* and *watermark*.

67

GA1321

Smokey the Stamp

Your job is to draw a stamp on this page, being very careful to follow the directions. Try to be as detailed as possible.

DIRECTIONS: The entire background should be done in very light shades of grey and should feature a bear's head, face and upper arm on the right side, as well as a ranger's hat that says "SMOKEY" in black print on top of the hat. On the front left hand, from top to the bottom, draw a tall dark brown branch which holds a small, realistic looking baby bear in shades of light and dark brown. In the bottom right-hand corner is written USA 20¢.

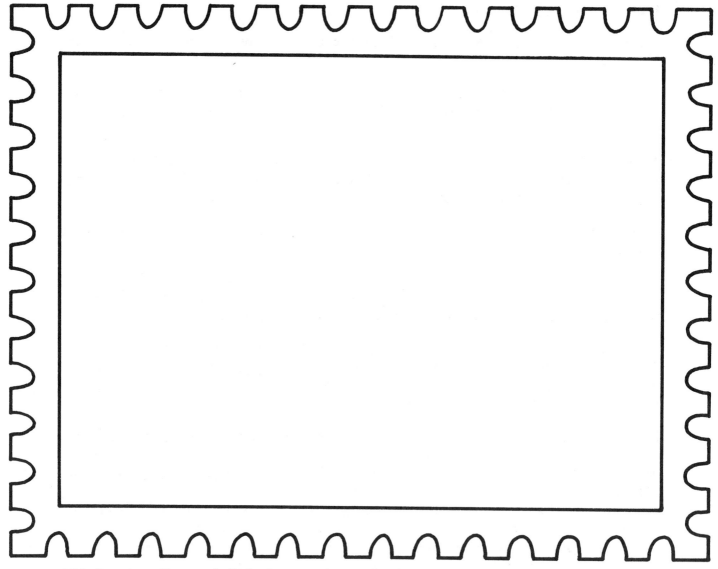

20¢ Smokey Bear—A little bear cub survived a devastating New Mexico forest fire in 1950 and became "Smokey Bear," symbol of forest fire prevention.

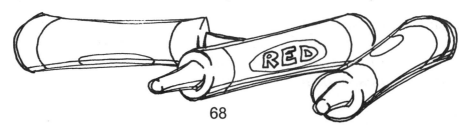

68

GA1321

Draw the Stamp

Draw a picture of a stamp that you think would commemorate each of the following events, people or things:

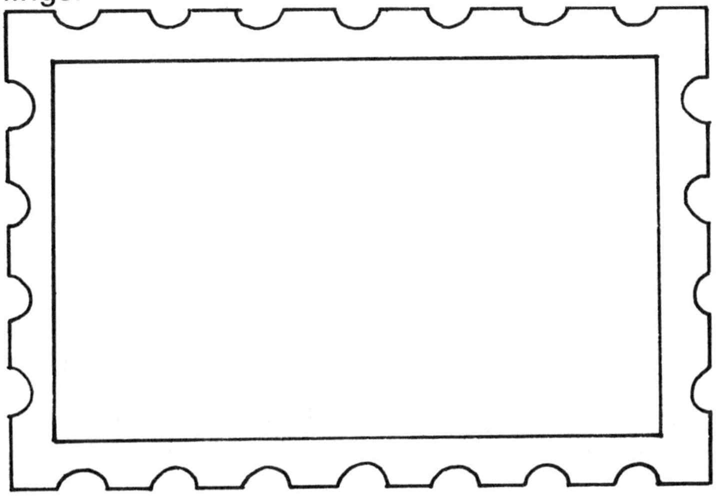

TAKE A BITE OUT OF CRIME
USA 20¢

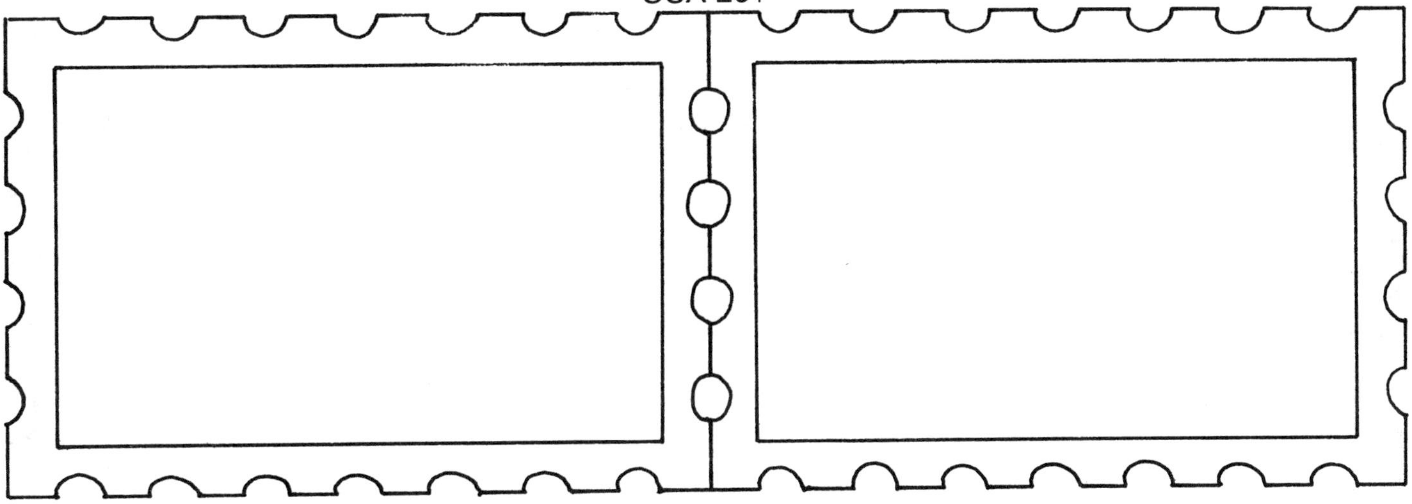

A NATION OF READERS
USA 20¢

SPECIAL OLYMPICS
USA 15¢

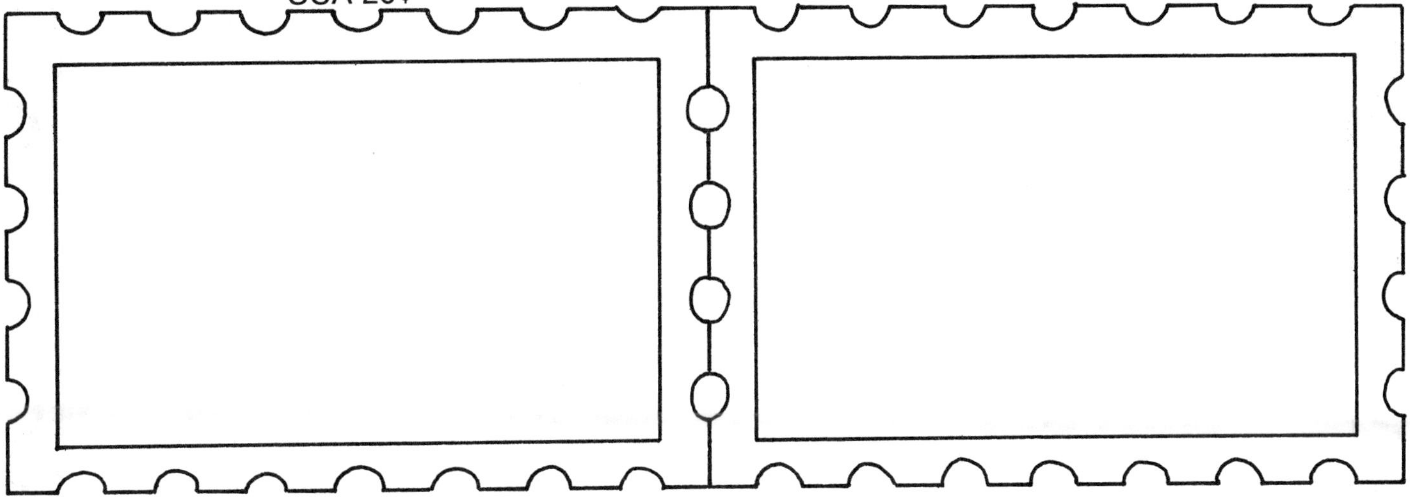

FIRST MAN ON THE MOON
10¢ AIRMAIL

BANKING COMMERCE
USA 10¢

GA1321

Collect Those Stamps!

For the next few days, ask your friends, neighbors, teachers and anyone else you can find to save all of their stamps for you. Try to collect at least twenty different stamps.

Now comes the hard part. Organize your twenty stamps by either size, shape, color or any other means you can think of. When your work is completed, glue the stamps onto this page and compare your collection to your classmates'.

CLASS PROJECT: Determine the monetary (money) worth of each stamp in your collection. Next, add the value of all your stamps together. Then compare and see who in your class has the twenty stamps which were worth the most and they will win the "$1,000,000 Stamp Sweepstakes."

70

GA1321

Brain Boggling Balloons Week

Teacher Tactics

Setting the Stage: Pose the following to your class "How many of you have ever wanted to fly? Have any of you ever had the opportunity to ride in a hot air balloon? Well, this week we'll be taking a closer look at hot air balloons, their history and how they're used today."

Invite someone knowledgable about hot air balloons to class and conduct a ten to fifteen-question interview. After the person has left, write a thank-you letter which expresses at least five things each student learned from the interview.

Ask your class if anyone's family owns a hot air balloon. If not, call a few of the local balloon agencies and see whether anyone would be willing to let the class watch a balloon go from being flat to being fully expanded. Also, allow students some time to observe the inside of the basket, so they can draw a detailed illustration of a hot air balloon at a later time.

Recommend to the class the benefits of riding in a hot air balloon, as well as the hazards. What safety precautions should both the passenger and the "pilot" take?

Hold a game day where students design gameboards inside file folders which will teach their players all about hot air balloons.

After you have attended a hot air balloon festival with your class (or seen a video of a hot air festival), ask students to write articles for the newspaper stating each student's impressions of the festival.

Take the class on an imaginary balloon trip in their minds, and make them vividly aware of all the spots they cross over.

GA1321

Brain Boggling Balloons Week

Absolutely Adaptable Activities

Imagine you're up in a hot air balloon. What would all the things on the ground look like as you went up?

What are some of the events included in competition flying? After listing those in existence, create your own competitive event.

Joseph and Etienne Montgolfier are often called the Wright Brothers of ballooning. Make an outline which includes all the reasons why they have been given this title. Then transform the outline into a report.

Write an advertisement for a hot air balloon company.

Create a two-balloon vehicle. Draw a detailed illustration of what it might look like, and write instructions as to how it might work.

Write some journal entries that the French physicist, Jean Francois Pilatre de Rozier might have made in 1783.

Create a menu for a meal you might want to take on your hot air balloon ride.

Create a short television script for a new situation comedy which takes place entirely inside a hot air balloon. What are some of the possible episodes that might occur after the season opener.

List five ways that hot air balloons can be realistically used other than for entertainment rides.

What is an aeronaut? Research information about this profession and make a TV commercial advertising for new people to join the profession.

Invent and design a model, to scale if possible, of a hot air balloon. If possible, label the parts.

Use your imagination! While riding in a hot air balloon, use all five of your senses to create a poem about the experience. (I feel the wind's blowing my hair, etc.)

Make a time line of all the important dates in ballooning history.

Design a questionnaire and survey your school population to discover how many students or teachers have ever ridden in a hot air balloon, how they enjoyed the experience, etc.

What kinds of jobs does ballooning create? Make a list of each job and tell specifically the task involved.

Compose a song about the "Joys of Ballooning." Set it to music.

Using only tangram pieces, create a picture of a hot air balloon.

Brainstorm ten to fifteen words which have to do with hot air balloons and put them into a secret word search in the shape of a balloon.

Balloon Clubs

Write a letter to one of the nationwide Balloon Clubs and Associations, asking for free information about hot air balloons. A few of the clubs' addresses are

Balloon Club of America
P.O. Box 114
Swarthmore, PA 19081

Wind Drifters Balloon Club
2814 Empire Ave.
Burbank, CA 91504

The Lighter-Than-Air Society
1800 Triplet Blvd.
Akron, OH 44306

GA1321

It Lost Control!

Write a short story about the hot air balloon that lost control. What did it do? Where did it go? Who was riding in it at the time? How did it all end? Include as many details as possible.

74

GA1321

A Balloon with a Different Face

Combine a balloon with another type of vehicle, such as a giant skateboard, a train, a surfboard, etc. See what kind of new vehicle you can come up with. Draw your new invention below and explain how it works.

GA1321

Have a Heart Week

Teacher Tactics

Setting the Stage: Pose this to your class: "How many of you think you have a heart? Besides the one in your chest, how many other ways are hearts used in our society? This week you will learn about the heart and the blood inside your body, along with a few other things."

If you could lay the blood vessels in your body end to end, there would be more than 100,000 miles of tubes! Go over this and other interesting facts about the circulatory system with your class.

The heart is about the size of a clenched fist. Brainstorm with your class all the other things that are also that size.

Reports about the heart might be done. Consider the following topics: the aorta, the pericardium, an atrium, the ventricles, the septum, an electrocardiogram, a stethoscope, varicose veins, a sphygmomanometer, hypertension, hemoglobin, immunity, a transfusion, a stroke, angina and cholesterol.

The Red Cross accepts blood donors. Call your local Red Cross and interview one of the staff about the blood collected and what happens to it and share the results with your class.

GA1321

Have a Heart Week

Absolutely Adaptable Activities

The heart can tell _____. Hearts are for _____.

Your heart is one of the most important parts of your body. Name ten other things that are really important to your health.

Doctors use a unique instrument called a stethoscope to listen to your heart. Find out all you can about this instrument.

If you knew someone had a bad heart, would you treat him any differently? Why or why not?

Your heart is a pump. Name all the other things you can think of with a pump or that pumps.

The heart is made of muscle. Research the heart and find out all you can about this important muscle.

If someone had a heart attack and was very weak afterwards, how would you cheer him up?

A grown-up's heart beats about seventy times a minute. If someone lives to be 75, how many times would that person's heart have beaten?

When the heart beats, it pushes blood into the tubes which carry it to all parts of your body, and that makes you have a pulse. See if you can find your pulse with an adult's help.

The tubes through which the blood goes to the heart are called veins. The tubes that take blood away from the heart are called arteries. The smallest tubes that blood goes through are called capillaries. Name everything that has tubes.

Oxygen is needed for every person to live. The blood carries the oxygen throughout the body. Brainstorm all the things that carry items from one place to another.

Platelets help your blood to clot when you bleed. They go to the cut and blend with special substances in the blood. Long, yellow threads form which cause a clot. This clot makes a plug that stops the bleeding. Finally, a scab is formed. Name all the coverings you can think of.

Name as many ways as you can that the word *heart* or *hearts* is used in our world.

Imagine you work in the heart section of the hospital. What are some of the jobs you might find there?

77

GA1321

Hearts on Fire

The heart symbolizes a lot of different things in our society. We have a holiday almost completely devoted to hearts. We have any number of bumper stickers stating I ♡ you, I ♡ my dog and I ♡ school. We have red, rainbow and speckled heart stickers to decorate books. Brainstorm all the ways the heart symbol could be used.

GA1321

Heart Research

The heart is the most important muscle in our body, and yet sometimes we abuse it by eating foods with cholesterol, by smoking cigarettes and by not exercising.

Talk to a doctor, your local Red Cross or the American Heart Association to find out as much as you can about the heart, how to keep it healthy and what things *not* to do. If you need more information, contact your school or public library for a wide range of books about the heart.

Copyright © 1991, Good Apple

GA1321

Heart Multiplication

a.　42 hearts
　　x 51
　　　　hearts

b.　63 aortas
　　x 39
　　　　aortas

c.　71 arteries
　　x 21
　　　　arteries

d.　86 atria
　　x 37
　　　　atria

e.　94 capillaries
　　x 61
　　　　capillaries

f.　23 lymph nodes
　　x 59
　　　　lymph nodes

g.　68 macrophages
　　x 74
　　　　macrophages

h.　42 pericardiums
　　x 51
　　　　pericardiums

i.　99 veins
　　x 44
　　　　veins

j.　33 platelets
　　x 12
　　　　platelets

k.　66 stethoscopes
　　x 72
　　　　stethoscopes

l.　89 ventricles
　　x 19
　　　　ventricles

GA1321

Holiday Happenings Week

(Month of December)

Teacher Tactics

Setting the Stage: Pose the following to your class: "What holiday is coming soon? That's right, Christmas! This week we have some interesting ways to look at Christmas and some things that you may never have seen or made before. Now, let's get started."

Use a dinner plate as the base for the Christmas centerpiece. Twisted snowflakes, tinfoil, popcorn balls, mistletoe, construction paper and any other colorful things you can find lying around the house or classroom can all be glued or tied to the center of the plate and then sprinkled with glitter for a little zest.

For the twelve days before Christmas vacation, impose on different students to share Christmas secrets as well as arts and crafts ideas that their families have used for years. Ask each student to bring in a sample of his idea to visually share with the class.

From Judith Hoffman Corwin's book *Christmas Fun,* here is a list of how to say "Merry Christmas" in many different languages.

Zalig Kerstfesst	Belgium
Shen Tan Kuai Loh	China
Glaedelig Jul	Denmark
Happy Christmas	England
Hauskaa Joulua	Finland
Joyeux Noel	France
Froehliche Weihnachten	Germany
Eftihismena Christoughenna	Greece
Nodlaig'mhaith chugnat	Ireland
Buon Natale	Italy
Feliz Navidad	Mexico
Hartelijke Kerstgroeten	Netherlands
Gledelig Jul	Norway
Boze Narodzenic	Poland
Boas Festas	Portugal
Sarbatori Vesele	Romania
Hristos Razdajetsja	Russia
Felices Pascuas	Spain
Gud Jul	Sweden
Nadolig Llawen	Wales

GA1321

Holiday Happenings Week

Absolutely Adaptable Activities

Long ago, it was a popular custom to present presents during festive occasions. The wealthy would give gifts to the commoners, and in return would receive wreaths of shiny leaves and incense. Try and imagine three other kinds of gifts that might have been given.

If you could have three wishes for Christmas, what would they be?

As a special part of Christmas, the Christmas stocking has been hung for more than 100 years. The children are anxious for Santa to bring them small gifts. Make a list of ten different presents that could fit inside a stocking.

In Holland, the little boys and girls put out their wooden shoes to be filled with presents. In other countries, very different kinds of stockings, both simple and very decorative and perhaps other types of gift holders (for example, sneakers) have been presented on Christmas morning. Brainstorm all the kinds of gift holders there might be.

What if Christmas came and there was only one present under the tree? What would it be? Why?

Wreaths of holly, mistletoe and pine have for many years been part of the Christmas festivities. What are some uses for these pieces of greenery?

Find a copy of the play *The Nutcracker* (you can find a great one in the book *Christmas Fun),* and with the students prepare it for the class.

The Christmas fairy is going to visit you this Christmas. What would you say to her?

Christmas cards were first done in the 1840's and are a huge part of holiday festivities today. They help us stay in touch, some add humor, while others add thoughtful sentiments to what might be an otherwise humdrum day. Create a beautiful Christmas card for someone you love.

England has mistletoe balls, the United States has puffed rice molasses balls and the Caribbean has benne balls. Name all the different kinds of balls you can think of.

The Caribbean creates a gourd noisemaker for its festivities. Name every way to make sounds that you can think of.

In China small peacocks made of bright colored feathers and chenille stems and balls are sent to other countries for Christmas. Name all the birds that you can brainstorm.

Write a recipe for a Christmas surprise.

GA1321

Christmas Multiplication

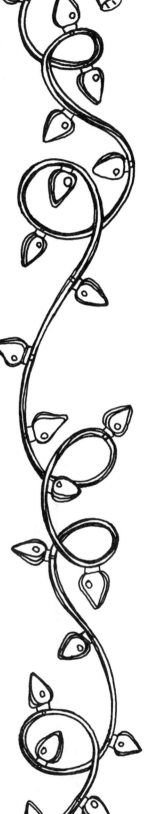

a.   67 lights
   x 8
   _____ lights

b.   83 hollies
   x 6
   _____ hollies

c.   42 mistletoes
   x 5
   _____ mistletoes

d.   91 trees
   x 4
   _____ trees

e.   79 decorations
   x 7
   _____ decorations

f.   36 icicles
   x 8
   _____ icicles

g.   29 cookies
   x 3
   _____ cookies

h.   19 candy canes
   x 6
   _____ candy canes

i.   51 gifts
   x 9
   _____ gifts

j.   72 wrappings
   x 4
   _____ wrappings

k.   63 projects
   x 7
   _____ projects

l.   14 angels
   x 8
   _____ angels

m.   58 carolers
   x 2
   _____ carolers

n.   87 snowflakes
   x 5
   _____ snowflakes

GA1321

Christmas Surprise Guest

It's Christmastime, and the snow is falling outside. The Christmas tree is lit and full of ornaments. The fire is burning in the fireplace, and the presents are under the tree. All of a sudden, there's a visitor at the door . . . .

Now you finish this story.

GA1321

Christmas Scene

Draw a very detailed Christmas picture below. Then with a pencil, "hide" at least ten candy canes in the picture. Finally trade your picture with a classmate and find each other's candy canes. Good luck!

85

GA1321

Dr. Martin King, Jr., Week

Teacher Tactics

Setting the Stage: Pose the following to your class: "Several years ago there was a strong man who believed that all people were born equal and therefore should be treated equal. This man's name was Dr. Martin Luther King, Jr., and he was a great leader. This week we will study about Dr. King and some of the things that happened during his time."

"I say to you today, my friends, so even though we face the difficulties of today and tomorrow, I still have a dream. It is a dream deeply rooted in the American dream . . . I have a dream. I have a dream that my four little children will one day live in a nation where they will not be judged by the color of their skin but by the content of their character . . . Let freedom ring from the snowcapped Rockies of Colorado! Let freedom ring from the curvaceous slopes of California! But not only that; let freedom ring from the Stone Mountain of Georgia! Let freedom ring from Lookout Mountain of Tennessee! Let freedom ring from every hill and every molehill of Mississippi. From every mountainside, let freedom ring."

Dr. Martin Luther King, Jr.

If appropriate, read the above quote, then ask your students to describe what *freedom* means to them in an essay.

If they could have any dream they wanted, and not one for themselves, what dream would each of your students choose? Ask each to write a poem to express his thoughts.

Ask students to imagine that for most of their lives they have been slaves and definitely not free. They have had no freedom to vote, to choose their own clothing or food; they were looked down upon by even their peers and then one magical day, it happened! They were free! Free to believe as they chose, free to walk down the street with their heads held high, free to use public transportation as they liked, free, free, free! Ask students to express verbally all the things that come to their minds if this were to really happen. And then ask them to express their feelings on paper in an essay.

GA1321

Dr. Martin King, Jr., Week

Absolutely Adaptable Activities

Do you think that it's important that we're all treated equally? Why or why not?

Dr. Martin Luther King, Jr., had a marvelous gift when it came to speaking ability, and his many speeches were listened to by even individuals who didn't agree with him. Write and give a speech to your class on a controversial topic that you firmly believe in.

If you knew that some other child was being treated unfairly, what would you do?

Dr. Martin Luther King, Jr., stressed nonviolence. There were many others who thrived on violence, and it was violence that ended Dr. King's life when at the age of 39, an assassin shot and killed him. Some historians believe his death ended the Civil Rights Movement he had fought so hard to maintain. If King had been spared his life, what other accomplishments might he have made?

Dr. King believed strongly in the weapon of protest, rather than violence. If you don't believe something is right, make a list of all the nonviolent things you can do.

Imagine you are a doctor and are asked to help a sick man, but your hospital doesn't want you to because he is of a different color. Would you help him anyway? Why or why not?

The Civil Rights Movement moved steadily after a woman named Rosa Parks sat in the white section of the bus and eventually got the Blacks to boycott (refuse to use) the use of all the buses. Eventually, the Supreme Court of Montgomery made the ruling to provide equal integrated seating on public buses. Do you think if Rosa Parks had not refused to sit in the black section of the bus, they might still be sitting there today? Write a theme stating your opinion.

What does it mean by the statement "And they all should be equal"? Equal in what ways? How many ways are there to be equal? Make a list. Are humans today equal in all those ways? Why or why not? When do you think they will be? Or should they?

Write a name poem about Dr. Martin Luther King, Jr., by writing his name vertically and then using the letters in his name to begin adjectives or nouns that describe Dr. King and his accomplishments.

As a child, Dr. King skipped two grades as he was going through school. He went on to college after the age of 15. What does this tell you about Dr. King? Research and then write a biographical outline about Dr. King's life.

GA1321

A Biographical Name Poem

The following is Martin Luther King, Jr.'s, name written vertically. You are to use each of the letters in his name to begin an adjective, a noun or a statement that describes Dr. King or his accomplishments.

M

A

R

T

I

N

Leader of the Civil Rights Movement

U

T

H

E

R

K

I

N

G

88

GA1321

King

```
                O G S
              V D Y B W
              H O F C M
              N L S H O
            U O J R A M C
            K N Z U D I V
            T R H E D N I
          J T R F L G I S A
          V Z H J V Q S I B
          C E Q F K C T O N
        M D K O L N B E N Q M
        B J G C W I G R B L Z
K N Z C B X D J R J C T B Q T D V P P R E J U D I C E C P R E A C H E R P J V
N P B X T F Z F X Y D G L S E B W I L E A D E R H S G L F T N W B K T N V
  I V L F V U D T P X G V M W Z G D L D G U V K A G X F J M X E Z H
  V J X Z L X C J Z B G O X Y J O F M N V E A S O T U N J X K E
    H V L R U C J F M N R E Z C K T Z T B N S V Q I J F E
    V K T L B R I S F S N K H Q W V L T A U C B D
      U C T B Q T R D H A H T R C A W S C K
      D T H X R J X V L R Z Q C C B S T
      C T Z D A W G X K E D C B K T I F
        I Q N T V R G I D D R E A M N
      T K O Z I B H N C K B V X V A A G
      B T U D O H Z X V F L J F L W T Z
      L O N T N P F V B Z F K R Z C E H
    L J Q V F S A Z J A O Q N P I V D B G
    J K F O V T C I B M Z B I O B J O N O
  W S W B Y S E G R E G A T I O N E U R G K
    O F G O X N O N V I O L E N C E G E P L F
    Q H G Q G K D C R F L   W N K V U G X E O B M
    J S L O F J X L T K     W Q S M V K A G H S
    T F G I X E I Z J W      H O I V P C W P Z W
    D F B G V W R O          J T K E E L G D F
    N D L V W L I J          E W C L F J B E
    G J P H N K E            B K O N E P H
    A V W T V G R            F E P R F W Z
    C N V U D                Z H O B L
    G T H V D                U R W R L
    F W K V                  W M Z L
    J T M N                  Z T C T
```

The following words can be found hidden across and down in the puzzle above.

DEMONSTRATION	ASSASSINATED	SEGREGATION
NONVIOLENCE	PREJUDICE	MINISTER
PREACHER	VISION	LEADER
PEACE	BLACK	DREAM

89

Two Great Leaders

Research both Dr. Martin Luther King, Jr., and Nelson Mandela. Make a list of all the ways they are alike and all the ways they are different.

GA1321

Mystery Monsters of the Deep Week

Teacher Tactics

Setting the Stage: Pose the following to your class: "Deep in the ocean, lies many mysteries and many creatures of which we aren't aware. This week, we'll be examining some of those creatures and discovering more about them. Now, let's get started."

West Indian manatees, or sea cows, were once believed from a distance to be mermaids. These mammals are related to the elephant and can grow to be as much as three to four (2.7 to 3.6 t) tons. Find out more about these interesting animals and publish a "sea cow or manatee newsletter" with your class.

The practically invisible sea wasp is one of the deadliest creatures of the sea. Once it stings, its victim is dead within a few minutes. The sea wasp is in the jellyfish family and lives off the coast of Australia. Write a class song which warns perspective victims of its deadly danger.

The blue whale is certainly the largest animal, both on land and sea, weighing up to 150 tons (135 t) and measuring up to 100 feet (30.4 m) in length. These whales are mammoth and immense, just to cite two adjectives. Brainstorm with your class all the other adjectives you can think of to describe the blue whale.

In 1963 in the Atlantic Ocean off of New Jersey, a fifty-foot (15.2 m) long creature called a ribbonfish was spotted, making it the longest known fish specimen ever recorded. Imagine that a new food was available to fish in the ocean that allowed them to grow to be this size. With the class, make a detailed prediction of the chain of events which might occur.

Visit an underwater aquarium and examine the sea creatures presiding there. Discuss the different species.

Invite an expert in water creatures to your classroom to give a small lecture. Then engage in a question and answer session.

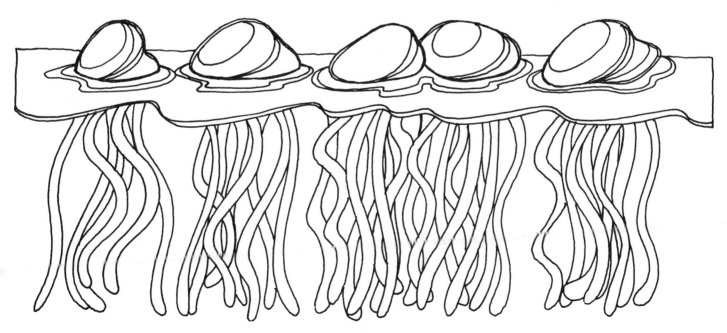

91

GA1321

Mystery Monsters of the Deep Week

Absolutely Adaptable Activities

In 1976 a giant creature was pulled up with an anchor. The creature had mistaken the anchor for bait and gotten stuck. It weighed 1650 pounds (742.5 kg) and was 14½ (4.41 m) feet long and they nicknamed it "Megamouth." The scientists believed it to be a member of the shark family, but it was the very first of its kind to have ever been found. Its mouth was luminescent and could light up the ocean floor. Write your own adventure about a similar shark.

What is the most unusual underwater creature you've ever seen in movies, books or in person? Draw it.

In April 1977, a large dead creature was pulled from the depths, weighing two tons (1.8 t) and reaching approximately 32 feet (9.76 m) in length. The body resembled the dinosaur plesiosaur, while the head and neck reminded some of the Loch Ness Monster or possibly a sea serpent. To this day, no one is really sure just what the creature was. But one morning imagine you go outside to your pool and there it is! Alive in your pool! Write out your plan of action and share it with the class.

Imagine you are going on an underwater fishing trip. Write about what happens when you pull up the hook.

A great white shark, the most deadly to humans, was captured in 1950 and was 21 feet (6.39 m) long and weighed 7100 pounds (3195 kg). This is the same shark that the shark in *Jaws* was modeled after. Write a TV script for a sitcom which contains a "Jaws-like" shark.

The Portuguese man-of-war is another type of dangerous sea creature. These animals wrap their bluish-purple tentacles around the victim and inject poison, causing severe cramping and pain. Write a "Watch Out" handbook for beach walkers, joggers and swimmers.

Monster worms, 8½ feet (2.59 m) long and pinkish with brilliant red tips or crowns, were found in the Galápagos Rift. Imagine that millions of these worms infiltrated your city. Write a scary story about what happens.

A little ways from Japan, a threadlike animal called a pogonophoran exists inside a skinny, transparent tube, which protects it from weather, enemies or just serves as a home for the animal. Make a list of twenty different animals and their habitats.

Design a game of Creepy Creatures Under the Sea by collecting information about these creatures in the library.

Choose five mysterious creatures and write a poem about each.

GA1321

And the Critic's Choice?

A new mystery creatures' movie has come to town, but no one has yet heard the title or really, for that matter, anything about it.

You are an undercover newspaper movie critic and your job is to find the title and description of this creepy creatures' flick and report back to us. Be as specific as possible.

Then give us your "critic's choice,"—thumb's up or thumb's down. Will this be a winner or not?

GA1321

A Potpourri of Thinking Activities

1. A smooshy, gooshy creature came out of a hole in the ground and ate 10 swichy giships, 5 wimbuy mimbies, 11 simons crimons and 3 unies bunies. When he was finally full, he crawled back into his hole and slept for three years. The question is, how many total critters did the smooshy creature eat during his visit above ground?

2. In three minutes, name as many things that begin with the letter *C* as you possibly can.

3. If monster worms were 8½ feet (2.59 m) long, and if sea wasp oddities were 4 feet (1.22 m) longer, and if phantom freaks were 11 feet (3.34 m) longer than that, how long were the phantom freaks?

4. Take the words *Mysteriously Creepy Creatures,* and in ten minutes try to find as many words as possible using only the letters as many times as they are presented in these three words (for example, treat).

5. Compose a name poem by writing *CREEPY CREATURES* vertically and then writing a word that begins with each letter that has to do with the title.

C
R
E
E
P
Y

C
R
E
A
T
U
R
E
S

94

GA1321

Creature in the Backyard

You have been plagued in your backyard by a type of creature who constantly makes gurgling noises and moves around in the night. You've turned to the exterminator, but he can't seem to get rid of it. You're not willing to stop yet. Brainstorm below at least ten different ways you can possibly remove the creature.

1.

2.

3.

4.

5.

6.

7.

8.

9.

10.

I'm Going Ape over You! Week

Teacher Tactics

Setting the Stage: Pose the following to your class: "Have you ever been to the zoo or read a book that had pictures of monkeys, gorillas, orangutans or chimpanzees? This week we're going to learn more about the great apes and other monkeys! Let's get started!"

The larger anthropoids—gorillas, orangutans and chimpanzees—are called the great apes. Ask students to write short oral reports about these apes.

Invite a zookeeper to your classroom who is knowledgeable about monkeys and great apes. Plan questions in advance and assign students to ask each one. After he's gone, brainstorm what was learned and write thank-you notes.

If you have a good zoo nearby with the primates on exhibit, take the class on a trip. Apes and monkeys are some of the most fascinating creatures to watch. Make sure students study closely the primates' movements and actions. Come back to the classroom and discuss what was seen and what conclusions can be drawn.

I'm Going Ape over You! Week

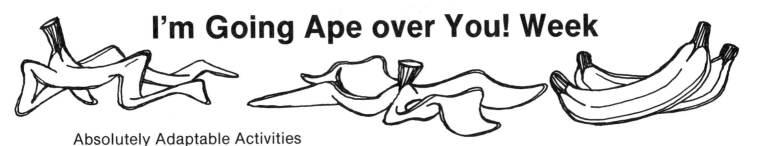

Absolutely Adaptable Activities

The gibbons and siamangs are called the "lesser apes." Write five reasons why they might have been given this name.

The gray skin of orangutans is tinged in blue. Compose a "Blue is . . ." ten-line poem.

Gorillas eat tough and stringy plants, gibbons feast on fruit and orangutans eat meat, plants and fruit. Design a menu for a restaurant which caters to all primates.

Pygmy chimpanzees are the most intelligent animals next to man. Research all the work that has been done with chimps and arrange a documentary for the class.

Imagine you had an ape for a pet, a chimp to be exact. How would you care for it?

A family of orangutans has moved into your neighborhood. Do you welcome them, or try to make them go away? Write a story.

Orangutans are often called "escape artists" by zookeepers around the world. They often open up their own cages just for the fun of it. Imagine a zoo with twenty orangutan cages, and one night all twenty apes open their cages simultaneously and . . . . Now, you finish the story!

Gorillas yawn, huff, cough and hiccup just like people. Put together a song, made up of gorilla noises and gestures, that a gorilla might chant.

When mature male gorillas pound their chests, it is either a threat or a sign of curiosity. When young gorillas beat their chests, it's an invitation to play. Make a list of all the body language signals humans put out for different things—jealousy, confrontation, insecurities, nervousness, hostility, happiness, etc.

Show the history of the ape and his relationship with man using a collage art form.

There are many different kinds of gibbons. Research the following: Kloss's Gibbon, White-Handed Gibbon, Dark-Handed Gibbon, White-Cheeked Gibbon, Silvery Gibbon and Grey Gibbon.

All the great apes, as well as the lesser apes, are on the endangered species list. Since most monkeys have no natural enemies, how do you explain their possible extinction?

Create a mobile, displaying all of the great apes and gibbons.

Draw a detailed diagram of a monkey and label all of its parts.

An orangutan is _____. A chimpanzee is _____
A gorilla is _____.

GA1321

Monkey Math

Add the following problems.

a.   9 primates
    + 3
    —————
        primates

b.   4 marmosets
    + 2
    —————
        marmosets

c.   10 tamarins
    + 5
    —————
        tamarins

d.   4 capuchins
    + 3
    —————
        capuchins

e.   7 douroucoulis
    + 6
    —————
        douroucoulis

f.   5 howlers
    + 6
    —————
        howlers

g.   4 spider monkeys
    + 2
    —————
        spider monkeys

h.   8 colobus monkeys
    + 4
    —————
        colobus monkeys

i.   7 guenos
    + 9
    —————
        guenos

j.   2 langurs
    + 6
    —————
        langurs

k.   5 macaques
    + 4
    —————
        macaques

l.   8 chimpanzees
    + 3
    —————
        chimpanzees

m.   9 orangutans
    + 6
    —————
        orangutans

n.   5 chimpanzees
    + 8
    —————
        chimpanzees

GA1321

Letter to World Wildlife Fund

Write a letter to the World Wildlife Fund, explaining to them your views about the endangered existence of the great apes and the monkeys. Write to:

World Wildlife Fund
1601 Connecticut Avenue, N.W.
Washington, D.C. 20009

GA1321

Silverback Gorilla Rules

The silverback gorilla is the strongest male in the gorilla group. Imagine that you are in a tropical forest and a silverback gorilla is coming towards you. What will you do? Make up five alternative solutions that will save you in this situation.

GA1321

Money—You Can Bank on It! Week

Teacher Tactics

Setting the Stage: Pose the following to your class: "How many of you think money is important? Why? Have you thought at all of coin collecting? Or what kinds of money are used in other countries? Well, this week we'll do an overview of money and delve into some of these questions."

Invite a professional coin collector into the classroom and ask him to share his collection as well as his expertise about the entire coin collecting hobby. Ask students to prepare questions to ask prior to the numismatist coming to your class.

Visit a coin collecting hobby store on a class field trip. Prepare interview questions prior to your arrival. Ask students to take notes and then hold a major discussion when you return back to the classroom.

Hold a coin collecting contest in your class. Each day, all the pennies brought in should be premarked and dated. Have a few pennies on hand for those who can't bring any. The object of the contest is to see which student can get as many pennies as possible dated in consecutive order from 1950. You decide on the length of time you'll devote to this week and day of the week, as well as when the contest is over. Hold a little ceremony in honor of the winner.

Challenge your students to start collecting coins on their own. It's easiest to start with pennies. Trying to find one penny for each year is a good way to start. Coins can be kept in any containers until students become serious enough to buy penny coin holders. All coin stores have them. Some students may want to collect nickels or dimes or if they are rich enough, even quarters. Some may want to investigate "proof sets."

GA1321

Money—You Can Bank on It! Week

Absolutely Adaptable Activities

What is a numismatist? Write for free information to:
Federal Reserve Bank of Atlanta
Atlanta, GA 30303

For counterfeit and fundamental facts about U.S. money, write to:
American Numismatic Association
818 N. Cascade
Colorado Springs, CO 80903

List ten reasons why money is so important to Americans.

Why is February 3rd, 1690, the First Issue of American Paper Money Day, so meaningful? What were monetary exchanges like prior to that time?

If you could buy only one thing in the world between now and when you die, what would it be and why?

Research the kinds of money they have in five other countries and share your information with the class.

Brainstorm ten things you would do if you suddenly won the lottery!

Interview five people and determine what role money has played in their lives.

Make a list of all the ways money is properly used.

Write a money mystery about Morley, the meanest money miser in Maine.

"Money can't buy happiness." "Money can't buy love." Interpret what these statements mean.

Write a fairy tale about the magical money tree and all its sense (cents).

Name all the ways money is used for the *wrong* reasons.

"Money doesn't make the man." Do you agree or disagree with this statement? Why or why not?

What might a scholar dollar be used for? How about a quarter porter? A sublime dime?

Collecting coins has been called the "hobby of kings." Coins have been around for over 2500 years. Imagine you were 2500 years old. Do you think you'd still be collecting coins? About how many do you think you'd have by then?

Brainstorm all the different places you might look for coins to collect (for example, couches).

All of a sudden, money isn't worth anything. The only things that have worth are peach pits. You need so many pits for a bike, so many pits for food, etc. You have to decide how many pits it will cost for ten different things.

Money, Moola, Cash, Stash!

1. A small eight-year-old boy named Bobby was getting an allowance for his coin collection. The first week he got 3 quarters and 5 dimes. The second week he earned 6 quarters. The third week he received 4 quarters, 7 dimes and one nickel. And, on the fourth week, he was given 200 pennies. How much total money did Bobby get for his coin collection over the four weeks?

2. Arnold loved coin collecting and every week for five weeks, he received 6 quarters, 11 dimes, 5 nickels, and 14 pennies. How much money did he receive over the five-week period?

3. Alex worked hard on weekends to earn enough money for his mother's birthday present. For four Saturdays in a row, Alex earned $2.50 per day. If his mother's present was going to cost $8.50, did Alex earn enough money? By how much?

4. One Sunday, Stevie found a $20.00 bill on his front driveway. He gave $10.00 to his Dad and bought four mini cars that were $1.75 each. How much money did he have left?

GA1321

You Won the Lottery!

You have just won the lottery and the prize is $1,000,000.00. The only catch is that you must *not* spend the money on yourself. You may only spend on others or for charities and donations to charitable organizations. Make a list of who the money will be given to and include how much each individual or group will get.

GA1321

The Family That Borrows

For your allowance, you have received $20.00.

Your mother needed to borrow $2.75 to go to the beauty parlor.

Your brother borrowed $1.35 for candy and gum.

Your dad asked to borrow $4.50 for the parking meter.

Your older sister had to borrow $3.40 for some makeup.

Your younger sister wanted to borrow $4.40 for school lunch.

Your aunt asked to borrow a quarter for a candy bar.

How much money do you have left?

Interesting Inventions Week

Teacher Tactics

Setting the Stage: Pose the following to your class: "How many of you have ever invented something? Let's discuss some of those inventions. What have been some truly great inventions over the past years? Why would you consider them great? Well, over the next week, we'll be talking a lot about inventions and inventors. Now let's get started."

Consider the old saying: "Necessity is the mother of invention." Discuss what this means with your class.

"I don't think necessity is the mother of invention; in my opinion it arises directly from idleness, possibly also from laziness—to save oneself trouble." Agatha Christie.

Compare and contrast the first and second quote with your students. Which one is true in your eyes?

The wheel was invented prior to 3000 B.C. Write a short class play about what it must have been like discovering the wheel. Finally, act it out for some other class at your school.

There are a few different reasons that items are invented—out of necessity, by accident, or a new use for existing inventions. As a class, compile examples of inventions which fall into each of these three categories.

As building progressed through the centuries, from tents to skyscrapers, different services were required for the interiors. Contact an interior decorator and ask him/her to come and talk with your class. Prepare a ten to twenty-question interview, including questions about the history of interior decorating, how it has changed through the years, specific job qualifications and descriptions, etc.

Louis Pasteur discovered "germs" and a process called pasteurization was named after him. Pasteurized milk is used for many different foods—ice cream, yogurt, cream cheese and cottage cheese, just to name a few. Have a PasteurOFF with your class! Ask each student to invent his/her pasteurized concoction, complete with name, description and directions for eating.

GA1321

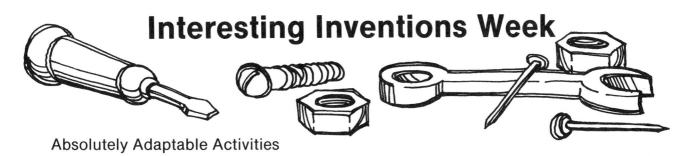

Interesting Inventions Week

Absolutely Adaptable Activities

Invent an imaginary potion that will make you jump incredibly high.

The invention of the steam engine began the Industrial Revolution in the 1700's. Research this time period and make a time line of the important events of that period.

Michael Faraday is often called the Father of Electricity. See if you can research a "father" of nuclear power, robots and computers.

Different plastics were invented, starting with celluloid in 1855, cellophane in 1912, and nylon in 1936, just to name a few. Find out the materials in plastic and how it is made. Then list all the different ways plastic is used in today's society.

Although most of us dislike housecleaning, it has been made a lot easier for us today through the use of inventions like vacuum cleaners and washing machines. Think about the housework that you and your parents do, then design at least one new machine to help with your work. Prepare a detailed diagram and explanations to share with your class.

Invent a cure for the disease videoitis.

King C. Gillette invented the safety razor, and the Kellogg brothers gave us breakfast cereals. Find out the "secret of their success."

The first zipper fastener was invented in 1891 by Whitcomb Judson. List twenty new and unusual uses for zippers. (Zip up a talkative mouth.)

Travel became easier and faster through the use of these inventions: the hot air balloon in 1783, the steamship in 1807, the steam railroad in 1830, the motor car in 1885, and the airplane in 1903. Other than a spaceship, design a vehicle of the future. Make a blueprint and/or a model of the new vehicle. Explain to the class how it works.

Edison invented the phonograph in 1877, and the engineers built the first music synthesizer in 1953. Because of these great inventions, you are able to hear the popular music of today. Compose an original song or make a collection of segments of already existing songs, and make a tape recording to share with the class.

Study one of the great inventors—Leonardo da Vinci, Benjamin Franklin, Alexander Graham Bell, Thomas Edison, George Washington Carver, the Wright Brothers or any other inventor you are interested in. Write a brief biographical poem or sketch of his or her life. Present it to the class in first person, and dress up like the inventor. Props might add to the performance.

Imagine all people are gone from the earth. Invent a machine to bring them back.

Create an advertisement to show off a new invention you've created.

Have I Got an Invention for You!

There have been quite a few inventions that never were accepted by the U.S. Patent Office such as eyeglasses for chickens, a spanking paddle with a safety feature, an alarm clock that hits your head and a fake tooth for good breath. Most of these inventions have been totally forgotten.

Your job is to create an invention that is so far-out and wild that it will probably be a big hit! You can combine two or three things into one, or create an answer to a question about which not many people think. Add a little humor and voila! You've got an invention which may never be forgotten!

GA1321

Create an Invention

Bertrum Snigleurts, a very intelligent scientist working on inventions, was trying to design a robot that helped one to exercise. The problem was that Bertrum was on a low budget, and he had only four materials with which to work. See if you can help him create an exercising robot with the following four objects:

SURFBOARD + BOWLING BALL + HELIUM-FILLED BALLOON + UNICYCLE =

109

GA1321

How Much Is That Invention in the Window?

1. Shorty made three inventions one day in his garage. Two of them each had 29 parts and the third invention had 16 parts. How many total parts did the inventions contain?

2. Peabody had a good time putting together his invention for a new flying fire escape. He needed 14 bolts, 24 nails, 26 screws, 3 washers and a large piece of wood. Peabody counted up all his supplies. How many were there?

3. A twirling spaghetti fork was being built by Tony Marsala, the Italian Pizza Parlor owner. The bateries cost $3.94, the fork cost $1.25 and the tape cost $2.97. How much money did Tony spend on the special fork?

4. A really unique robot was being built in the mind of Larry Terry, and he decided to check out the prices of the pieces. The body was going to cost $27.50, and the other accessories were going to add up to $39.41. If Larry were to make the robot, how much would it cost him?

Out of This World! Week

Teacher Tactics

Setting the Stage: Pose the following to your class: "Have you ever daydreamed that you were on another planet or in a spaceship orbiting the moon? Well, during this Out of This World Week we'll examine those who may have orbited the moon, we may talk to an alien or we may write rules for traffic jams in space."

February 20th is the day that honors the American astronaut who, in 1962, first orbited the earth. John Glenn circled the earth three times and then landed in the Atlantic. Assign research projects about how astronauts are selected, any kind of training of which they may partake, and women astronauts as well as Russian cosmonauts. Many short reports or several long ones may fulfill your goal. Information can be gathered in the form of outlines, essays, games or puppet shows.

Older students might choose to read John Glenn's autobiography to learn about John Glenn's life since he went into space. In addition, students could read about other astronauts and any physical problems they might have developed due to their extraterrestrial adventure.

Students can write for a chart titled "America's Twentieth Century Space Travelers," which is free from:
McDonnell Douglas
Box 516
Saint Louis, MO 63166

Write to the NASA Space Center in Langley, Virginia, to arrange for a telelecture. A slide show will be sent to you. On the scheduled date, a two-way telephone will be connected to your class and the Langley Space Center, and the Space Center will call you!

GA1321

Out of This World! Week

Absolutely Adaptable Activities

Write a far-out story about the mysteries of space.

Design a robot that will take over one of the spaceships, should something happen to the astronaut. Include all the duties it will have to accomplish to get the ship safely back to earth.

Make an "Out of Space" calendar for the year 3000.

Create a new cereal that space creatures would enjoy. Design the box, too.

Write a weather forecast for the planet Ico.

Compose a love note from one clone to another.

Construct a star station and a series of fighter spaceships who reside there.

Design a travel poster, mapping out directions from one planet to another.

Write ten traffic rules for spaceships.

Draw a detailed diagram of the inside of one of the space shuttles.

Design a space game, complete with board, tokens and information cards.

Display at least five different space vehicles on a poster, and then label their component parts. Write a compare-contrast essay between two of the five.

Create a space diorama, showing a war between two spaced-out planets.

Do a takeoff on one of the popular space serials like *Star Trek.*

Write a mystery about a newly discovered planet.

Using words related to space, design a secret word search in the shape of a rocket.

Using parts of theme songs from various space movies, create a new song for a roll-up movie you've designed.

Draw a picture of a spaceship.

GA1321

Isn't There a Thing to Eat?

Think about a NASA space flight to Mars. The flight will last for a long period of time. Create a daily diet for an astronaut team that will be traveling to Mars and back.

DAIRY PRODUCTS

MEAT PRODUCTS

VEGETABLES

FRUITS

DESSERTS

BREADS

GA1321

The Planet Ziba!

A new planet has been discovered and it has been named Ziba. One of the creatures from Ziba is coming to earth, and you have been given the task of interviewing the Ziba creature.

You'll need to decide on the ten best questions to ask and write those first. Then you'll need to *imagine* what the creature might answer and write those answers next to the questions. Good luck!

1.

2.

3.

4.

5.

6.

7.

8.

9.

10.

GA1321

The Martians Have Landed!

You work on a newspaper and a hot story has just hit your office! The Martians have landed in the United States, and you need to write the story telling all about what happened, using as many details as possible.

Don't forget to answer Who? What? Why? When? Where? How?

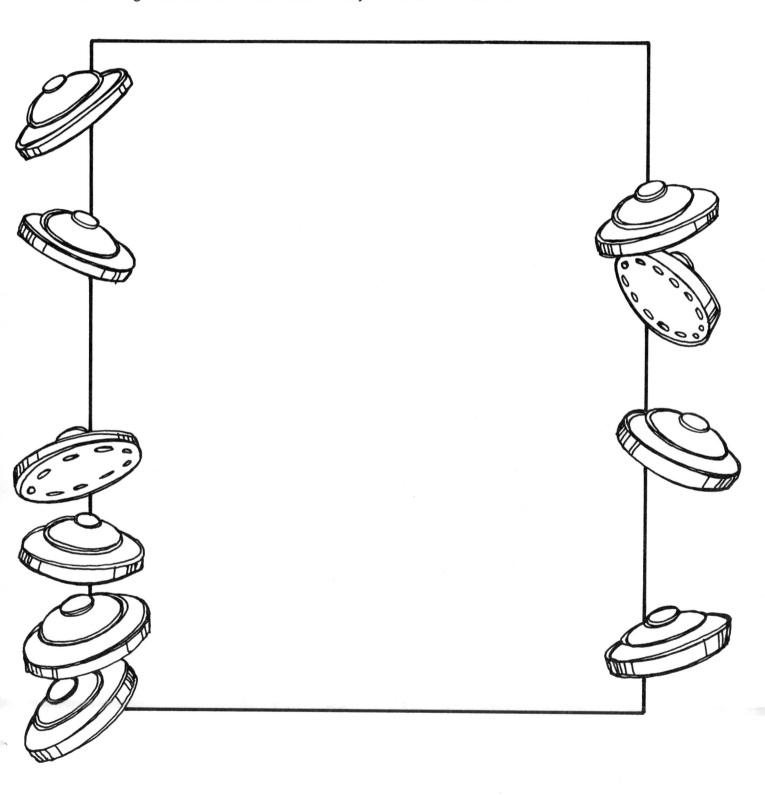

GA1321

Zooming to the Zoo Week

Teacher Tactics

Setting the Stage: Pose the following to your class: "Where can you find a large group of animals all in the same place? Some are big, some very small, but they all have to survive under the same weather conditions. Where? IN THE ZOO! This week we'll be focusing on the zoo and all of its different parts."

Visit your local zoo. Take a guided tour of the zoo. When you return, brainstorm reasons for having zoos. Rank your list, starting with the best reasons first.

Invite a zookeeper to your classroom to share all he knows about zoos. Ahead of time write a collection of questions to ask the zookeeper, and assign different students to ask the questions.

Draw and paint a class mural of a zoo scene.

Create a class collage of zoo animals.

Set up a Zoo Center in a corner of your classroom with a bulletin board and desk. Cover both with colorful butcher paper and use pictures of the students' favorite zoo animals as a background. Cover a box with some animal gift wrap and curtain hooks. Hang creative writing titles or extra credit tasks on each hook.

GA1321

Zooming to the Zoo Week

Absolutely Adaptable Activities

Take the legs of one animal, the head of another, the body of another and the tail of yet another. Give your new animal a name and write down five characteristics about it. Then do the same with ten to twenty more creatures and you've created your own zoo! Put the animals in "cages" and take the class on a walking trip past each one.

Make a twenty-six-card fact file about zoo animals, beginning each with a different letter of the alphabet. (Example: A is for aardvark; B is for baboon.)

Classify all the zoo animals you've seen in groups. Then make lists of all the things that members of each group have in common.

What if zebras could swim? Otters could roam? Anteaters could fly? What new qualities or characteristics would these animals need to do these things? Draw pictures and illustrate your ideas.

Paint a variety of wild animals and cut them out. Create a collage.

Make a list of ten warnings people should heed while at the zoo.

Design a wire sculpture of one of the wild animals you are studying.

Draw a poster of the oldest known animal.

Design a series of zoo postcards. Run off copies and sell them to your classmates.

Construct a jigsaw puzzle of an animal that lives in Africa.

Predict and make a model of what a zoo will look like in the year 3000.

Take slides of all the zoo animals. Write a one or two-sentence description of each and take the class on a slide trip to the zoo!

Take one of your favorite zoo animals and create a papier-mâché model of it.

Have you ever been to the zoo? Name five animals you saw.

Write a telegram to one of the zoo animals telling him you're coming to visit.

GA1321

A Brand-New Kind of Baby

Pretend that two very different animals, an anteater and a rhinoceros, meet, like one another and start a family! Draw a picture of what their babies might look like. Name them. Write a funny story about them.

GA1321

Create a Souvenir

Lots of different souvenirs are sold at the zoo, such as hats, cups, posters, etc. You are to create a souvenir unlike any other thought up before for the Wannebego Zoo. Draw a picture of this souvenir below.

119

GA1321

Prisoner Behind Bars

Animals sit for years behind the bars which enclose them. They sit, they stare, they pace and they prance. Haven't you ever wondered what they think of humans?

Imagine you are an animal shut behind bars! Write down eight things that you might possibly be thinking about those who stare at you, day in and day out.

GA1321

Setting Precedents with Presidents Week

Teacher Tactics

Setting the Stage: Pose the following to your class: "Who holds the highest position in our country? That's right—the President of the United States! What is his job? How much does he make per year? These questions and more will be answered during Setting Precedents with Presidents Week."

"The President of the United States is often considered the most powerful elected official in the world."

"The only thing we have to fear is fear itself." Franklin Delano Roosevelt. Have the class think about this statement and then write original poems entitled "What Fear Means to Me."

Put on a mock Inauguration Day ceremony, using classmates to help "set the stage." Read the Oath of Office and discuss its meaning.

Ask students to choose one of the presidential greats: George Washington, Abraham Lincoln, John Kennedy, etc. Ask each student to write a biographical sketch of the President he selected. Finally the student is to dress up as "him" and tell about "his" life to the class.

Harry S. Truman gave the order to drop the first and second atomic bombs on Japan. Discuss with your class how the course of history might have been altered had this not have happened.

Describe the presidential election process on a scroll you unravel and share with the class.

GA1321

Setting Precedents with Presidents Week

Absolutely Adaptable Activities

Thirteen officials make up the Cabinet. List what those thirteen executive positions are and give explanations of each.

Name all of the Presidents and ex-Presidents you can think of.

Thomas Jefferson drafted the Declaration of Independence in 1776. Find out why some consider this to be the most important document in American history.

One of the smallest Presidents, James Madison, stood only 5'4" (1.62 m) and weighed less than 100 pounds (45 kg). Research what other "short" Americans made their way to fame and glory. Make a list and describe each person's accomplishments.

Van Buren was nicknamed the "Little Magician," William Henry Harrison was nicknamed "Old Tippecanoe" and Zachary Taylor was nicknamed "Old Rough and Ready." Find out the nickname for each President, and then make up some of your own nicknames for the current President.

Two sets of relatives attained the presidency over the years—John Adams was the father of John Quincy Adams and Benjamin Harrison was the grandson of William Henry Harrison. How probable is it that two members of the same family would make it into the presidency in this day and age? Back up your answer with sound reasons.

Eli Whitney patented the cotton gin while George Washington was in office. Discover why this invention was so important to history.

President Tyler had fifteen children over the course of his life. Imagine that the White House was in the shape of a big shoe and poor President Tyler just didn't know what to do! What suggestions do you have for a President with fifteen kids who lives in a shoe?

The current presidential salary is $200,000 a year. If you had a budget of that much, how would you spend it? Make a list of the things you would get and do.

John Kennedy was one of the youngest persons to ever be elected President. Reagan was the oldest person to ever be elected President. Does age make any difference as to the quality of performance as President? Was Reagan any better President than Kennedy? Hold a class debate—one side arguing that age makes a difference in presidential quality, while the other side argues that age has nothing to do with how well a president will do.

Imagine you are President of the United States and have to make a very important decision. What would it be?

GA1321

Presidential Trivia

Answer the following questions as best you can. If you absolutely can't think of an answer, try the encyclopedia under "Presidents."

1. Who was the only President who did not win an election to become either Vice President or President?

2. Who was the largest President?

3. Who were the only grandfather and grandson who both served as President?

4. Which President never married?

5. Which Presidents lived past the age of 90?

6. Who was the only President to resign?

7. What two former Presidents died on the same day?

8. Who was the youngest person ever to become President?

9. Which Presidents died on the Fourth of July?

10. Who was the oldest person ever elected President?

GA1321

An Environmental Problem

You have been elected President for a four-year term. Within those four years, you have stated you will solve the national environmental problem. Your job is to map out your strategy, one idea at a time, until an overall solution can be reached to save the environment. The more ideas you can think of, the better.

Make a list of your ideas below. When you've listed ten to twenty different ideas, choose two that you feel are really great solutions. Then look at the pros and cons for each of the two. Finally make your decision and "road map" exactly what you'll do to save the environment. Good luck!

GA1321

A Presidential Situation Comedy

A brand-new situation comedy (sitcom) on television is set in the office of the President of the United States and revolves around the goings-on which take place at the White House. Your job as scriptwriter is to create a one-page script for the first scene of the sitcom. Try to make it as humorous as possible.

Pigs on Parade Week

Teacher Tactics

Setting the Stage: Pose the following to your class: "Think about a farm and all the animals that live there. What are some you can think of? A pig. Well, this week we're going to learn a little bit about the pig and what it eats, how it sounds at different times, and the care a mother pig or sow gives her young, among other facts about pigs."

Read to the class the book *Charlotte's Web.* What role did Wilbur the pig play? Have students create their own mini books with a domestic pig as the main character.

Visit a farm, if possible. Point out a sow, her piglets and a boar. Have students keep notes about what they see.

Go over definitions for *farrowing, litter, tusks, teats, snout, udder, sow, boar, birthing pen* and *weaned* in a "Pigs in the Know" dictionary.

"Pigs make superb mothers." Outline the care the mother sow gives her young during their first year of life.

Have a farmer visit your classroom. Discuss farming and pig raising.

GA1321

Pigs on Parade Week

Absolutely Adaptable Activities

If four pigs went to school and read two books apiece, how many total books would that be?

Write about what would happen if pigs became extinct.

Miss Piggy, the Muppet, has a very distinctive personality and voice. Design your own pig puppet, complete with a clever piggy monologue. Present a swine show.

What is the difference between a pig and a peccary? Make a compare-contrast chart listing their similarities and differences.

Pigs are believed by many animal experts to be highly intelligent and adaptable. Design at least one test which would determine whether or not this point is valid.

What are a piglet's and full-grown pig's daily diets like? Create a meal planner for a week.

The record weight for a full-grown pig was 1904 pounds (856.8 kg). Imagine yourself all that weight! Write a poem about how your life would be different.

State the difference between a piglet, pig, hog, boar, gilt, barrow and stag in a "Pig Starlight Guide."

The international language of the pig is grunting. Create a chant that pigs might grunt in glee, disappointment or aggression.

List ten uses for a pig's snout.

Truffles are very rich chocolate candies, but they are also very valuable fungi grown in France and Italy. This fungus is worth up to $2000 a pound (.45 kg). Pigs, with their incredible snouts, can sniff out the truffles which grow 12" (.30 m) underground, from twenty feet (6.1 m) away. With the pig's great sense of smell, name some uses for the pig in America.

Illustrate the history of the pig on a colorful time line.

In Orwell's *Animal Farm*, Napoleon, the leader of the pigs, was quoted as saying, "All animals are equal. But some animals are more equal than others." Explain what you think this statement means and whether or not you agree with it.

GA1321

Using the Pig

In addition to using the pig's meat for food, the pig's body is useful in many other ways. Research the pig in the encyclopedia to determine all the uses for a pig's body that there might be.

128

GA1321

Pigs on Calendars

Choose one of the following pigs and create a calendar page with its picture: Berkshire, Chester White, Duroc, Hampshire, Landrace, Poland China, Spotted Poland China, Tamworth or Yorkshire purebred pigs. (You'll need to research these pigs to find out specifically what to do to illustrate your calendar page, and it will also teach you a little bit about each chosen pig.)

Mother with Too Many

The record pig litter numbered thirty-four! Imagine an adult human mother who also bore thirty-four offspring! She didn't live in a shoe, but she did have so many children she didn't know what to do! Write a story with a lot of solutions for the mother included. Have fun!

130

GA1321

Ships, Ahoy Week

Teacher Tactics

Setting the Stage: Pose the following to your class: "What is the difference between a boat and a ship? What are some very famous ships? The answers to these questions and more will be coming your way during this Ships, Ahoy Week, so be prepared."

"We're just two ships that pass in the night. . ." Barry Manilow
Ask the class what they interpret this line to mean, and then have them write their own "shippy" songs.

There are many words that rhyme with the word *ship.* Brainstorm with the class all the one, two and three-syllable words that rhyme with *ship.*

In 3200 B.C., the Egyptians invented sails. With your class, brainstorm all the things for which sails could have been constructed.

The *Clermont,* built by Robert Fulton of the United States, became the first commercially successful steamboat. Hold a class contest to see how many different kinds of ships each student can brainstorm.

Francis Pettit Smith, an Englishman, and John Ericsson, a Swede, in 1836 patented propellers to drive steamboats. Take a few moments to discuss with your class all the various ways a propeller works.

Every day, ships sail the oceans, seacoasts and inland waterways. But they are just one type of transportation. Brainstorm with the class all the other types of transportation and place them in categories.

GA1321

Ships, Ahoy Week

Absolutely Adaptable Activities

Imagine you've invented a special kind of ship that can turn invisible. How would you use it?

Christopher Columbus sailed to America on board the *Santa Maria,* and followed with the *Nina* and the *Pinta*. However, these ships were small in comparison to modern-day vessels. Make a compare-contrast chart between the ships of old and those of the present.

Create a "Ships, Ahoy" eight-line poem.

Make up names for at least five ships—two large, one medium, two small.

A relatively new kind of oceangoing giant is the hydrofoil. Research this vessel and write a short oral report to share with the class.

The *Queen Elizabeth II* is one of the largest ships ever built. She is 963 feet (288.9 m) long and stocks enough ice cream for one transatlantic crossing to fill 224,000 single-dip cones. If you had a ship this large, how would you design it? Make a diagram and label all the parts.

In a vessel version of a dictionary, explain the following terms: *destroyer, battleship, submarine, tugboat, hydrofoil, steam turbine, cruise ship, cargo vessel, container ship, tanker* and *drilling rig.*

In a *Braving It in Boats* book, tell all you can find out about rafts, canoes, kayaks, rowboats, shells, sailboats, clippers, steamships, junks, catamaran fishing boats, dredgers, ferries and hovercrafts.

Invent a ship and draw a detailed picture of it.

Combine a canoe, a sailboat and a raft to create a brand-new craft.

A mystery took place aboard a Chinese junk. The only clues that were found to the robbery were one fingerprint on the ship's safe, a matchbook on the floor by the safe, and a broken glass scattered all over the floor. Write your version of what happened and solve the robbery.

Using the words *A Ship a Day Keeps the Doctor Away* try to make as many three-letter, four-letter and five-letter words as possible, using each letter only as many times as they are presented.

The British steamer named *Titanic* struck an iceberg on its first trip from England to New York City and sank. It took about 2½ hours to sink and there were about 705 survivors. If you were on a ship that you knew was going to sink in a short period of time, what would you do? How would you act? What things would go through your mind?

GA1321

A Ship's Adventure

An adventure occurred aboard the *USS Saratoga* one summer. Fifteen basketball players booked passage on the first of June and came aboard with only two things on their minds—exercise and relaxation.

But when they boarded, they were sent on an obstacle course all over the ship which never ended until they left the ship on June 12th.

Your job is to describe this obstacle course in great detail. Create an adventure story around it and don't stop until you finish! Good luck!

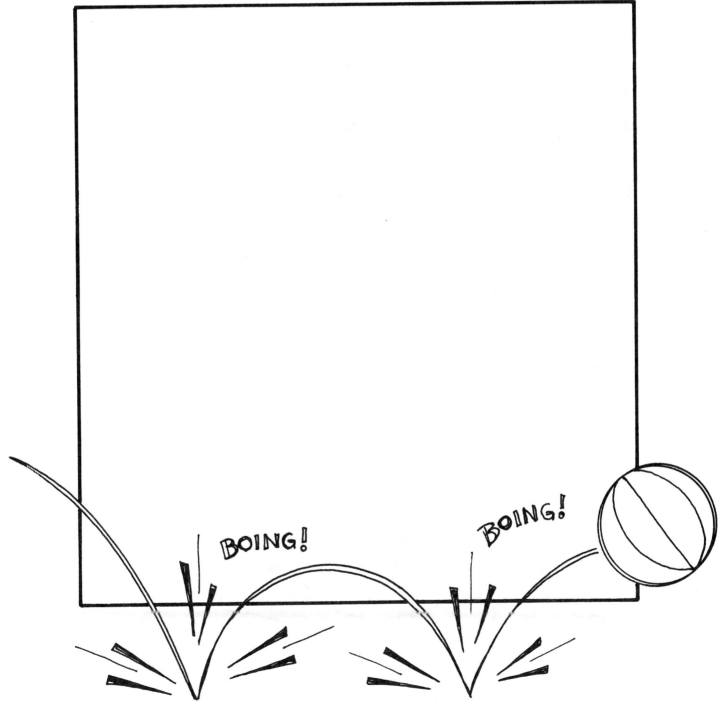

GA1321

Circle the Ship!

Circle each of the following which fits into the category of ships. If you're not sure, look it up in the dictionary.

CARGO VESSELS

FERRIES

CANOES

HYDROFOILS

HARBOR BOATS

SAIL SHIPS

LUXURY LINERS

AIR CUSHION VEHICLES

TANKERS

TRAMP SHIPS

TAXI SHIPS

CONTAINER SHIPS

LASH SHIPS

ROLL-ON/ROLL-OFF SHIPS

DRY BULK CARRIERS

MULTIPURPOSE SHIPS

OCEANOGRAPHIC SHIPS

REFRIGERATOR SHIPS

CLIPPER SHIPS

SYMINGTON SHIPS

LATEENER SHIPS

NUCLEAR-POWERED MERCHANTS

NORTHERN EUROPEAN COGS

FREIGHTERS

ITALIAN TWO-MASTED CARRACK

VIKING SHIPS

SPANISH GALLEONS

WARSHIPS

FULL-RIGGED SHIPS

ROMAN GRAIN SHIPS

ANCIENT SCANDINAVIAN HIDE BOATS

DUGOUTS

LOG RAFTS

RIVERBOATS

GALLEY SHIPS

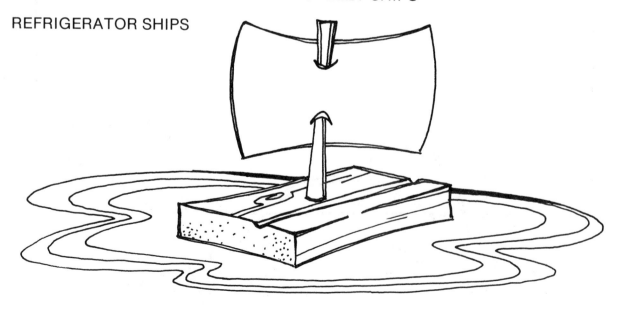

GA1321

A Ship's Day—Find the Answer!

Choose a word which will answer each of the following questions. Use the answers at the bottom of the page to help you.

1. One of man's oldest forms of transportation is _____.

2. Bad men who used to roam the seas were called _____.

3. Large oceangoing vessels are _____.

4. Long narrow boats powered by a row of paddlers are _____.

5. A ship's sails with masts and ropes is its _____.

6. To move swiftly is to _____.

7. A steam engine with two cylinders is _____.

8. The front part of a ship is the _____.

9. The rear part of a ship is the _____.

10. The ship's steering wheel is its _____.

Choose from these answers: compound, helm, galleys, bow, pirates, stern, rigging, ships, shipping, clip.

GA1321

Delving into Dinosaurs Week

Teacher Tactics

Setting the Stage: Pose the following to your class: "How many of you are interested in dinosaurs? Would you be interested in a week of activities dealing with dinosaurs? Well, during Delving into Dinosaurs Week, we'll make dinosaur sculptures, compose science-fiction dinosaur stories and do some dinosaur research, just to name a few of our activities."

Tell the class what an enormous industry the dinosaur paraphenalia business really is and how dinosaur paraphenalia can be found virtually everywhere. Brainstorm, as a class, all the different kinds of paraphenalia they've seen.

In the movie *Fantasia* by Disney, several dinosaurs romped together to the tune of Igor Stravinsky's "Rite of Spring." It might be fun for you to check out this album from a public library or music store or even to purchase it yourself to play while engaging in Dinosaur Week and all of its activities.

Create sculptures of triceratops, pteranodon, dimetrodon or tyrannosaurus rex out of aluminum foil and toilet paper rolls. Spray paint the finished products. Use black magic markers to add details. Fadeless art paper and pipe cleaners might also be added for more details.

Ask your students to create mobiles demonstrating dinosaurs with long legs.

There is a three-minute cassette tape called "Walk the Dinosaur" that you can purchase at record and tape stores. You might want to use it for a background to one or more of your activities.

Use any of the dinosaurs your students are interested in and interchange them with those on the next page.

Delving into Dinosaurs Week

Absolutely Adaptable Activities

Do you believe a dinosaur would have made a good pet? Write a paper telling why or why not.

Imagine you could talk to a tyrannosaurus rex. What would you say?

Create a diorama portraying leaf-eating dinosaurs in their natural habitat.

Design a bumper sticker that reveals your favorite kind of dinosaur.

Compare and contrast a pteranodon with a cactus wren in a chart of similarities and differences.

Deinoychus means "terrible claw." Imagine that a creature invaded your planet with a giant gross claw. Devise a rescue plan you would use to help save the world.

Make a twenty-five-card fact file about the four-legged dinosaurs.

Create a flip book which shows how dinosaurs changed over the years.

Compose a science-fiction story which discusses the supersaurus.

Tear out words from any paper or magazine and glue them onto construction paper to create three sentences about stegosauruses.

Design a scrapbook of at least five flying and swimming dinosaurs and five land dinosaurs by drawing pictures of each of these creatures.

Most horned dinosaurs had huge body shields on their heads. Name all the other methods of protection which dinosaurs had.

Some dinosaurs were carnivores or meat-eating and some were herbivores or plant-eating. Make a list of other types of animals who are both carnivores and herbivores.

Create a board game which focuses on the dinosaur theme and includes rules, tokens and a gameboard.

Make an advertisement for a Dinosaur Doughnut Shop in downtown Detroit. All the doughnuts and pastries are shaped like dinosaurs.

Make believe that a stegosaurus who was believed to be extinct was suddenly discovered in someone's basement. Write the story of the century.

GA1321

A Great Birth

During the conclusion of the Mesozoic Era, a lot of the plants and animals died. This period was known as the Great Death, and it happened quickly. Well, actually, it took less than a million years, if you want to call that quickly. But no one knows the exact amount of time since none of us were there!

For a few minutes, pretend that instead of a Great Death it was a Great Birth, and that man began to roam the earth, too. What do you see happening on the planet with the dinosaurs mixing with man? What kinds of problems might become of this? Write a short story below.

GA1321

Double-Digit Dinosaurs

a.   25 plesiosaurs
    + 47 ichthyosaurs
      dinosaurs

b.   89 pterosaurs
    + 23 ornithosuchuses
      dinosaurs

c.   51 thecodonts
    + 42 dromaeosauruses
      dinosaurs

d.   97 hypacrosauruses
    + 29 tyrannosauruses
      dinosaurs

e.   41 carnotauruses
    + 68 allosauruses
      dinosaurs

f.   54 dilophosauruses
    + 76 velociraptors
      dinosaurs

g.   81 gallimimuses
    + 26 acrocanthosauruses
      dinosaurs

h.   32 stegosauruses
    + 49 saichanias
      dinosaurs

i.   29 edmontonias
    + 64 euoplocephaluses
      dinosaurs

j.   95 daspletosauruses
    + 36 centrosauruses
      dinosaurs

k.   16 torosauruses
    + 14 stegosaurs
      dinosaurs

l.   53 sauropeltas
    + 67 apatosauruses
      dinosaurs

m.   21 camarasauruses
    + 44 diplodocuses
      dinosaurs

n.   63 supersauruses
    + 15 brachiosauruses
      dinosaurs

GA1321

Dinosaur Definitions

Write a one-sentence description of each of the following dinosaurs. (Example: tyrannosaurus rex—A large meat-eating dinosaur that could cut food with its teeth.)

ALLOSAURUS:

STEGOSAURUS:

TRICERATOPS:

SUPERSAURUS:

DIPLODOCUS:

BRACHIOSAURUS:

ICHTHYOSAUR:

PLESIOSAUR:

BRONTOSAURUS:

PTERONODON:

ELASMOSAURUS:

GA1321

Avid About Advertising Week

Teacher Tactics

Setting the Stage: Pose the following to your class: "Have you ever been driving down the street in your family's car when all of a sudden, you looked up and there was a giant billboard advertisement staring you right in the face? Or have you seen other advertisements on the sides of buildings, buses, benches, etc.? The world is filled with all kinds of advertisements, and this week we'll discuss a few."

Call a few local ad agencies and ask if your class can come for a tour. Students will be fascinated, especially with the art room. Ask them to write down all they've learned from the outing.

Invite one or two advertisers to the classroom to share with the class their knowledge and expertise about advertising. Allow time for questions and answers. Ask them back to view student presentations. The input will be good for the class.

Use the different magazine ads to create animal pictures. Cut out the ads, piece them together and create imaginary ad-animal pictures. Write funny stories about them at the bottoms of the papers.

Spend one day creating newspaper ads, one day on magazine ads, another day on billboard ads and a fourth day on Yellow Page ads.

Avid About Advertising Week

Absolutely Adaptable Activities

Research the art of advertising. How has it changed over the past twenty years?

Design a billboard advertisement for a new kind of tennis shoe.

Design a booklet of six different advertisements, each for a kind of paper towel currently on the market (Yellow Pages, magazine, newspaper, billboard, radio, and TV).

Write an advertisement for a new kind of dog food. Sell it to the class.

Write and illustrate a newspaper advertisement for a new children's toy.

Compose a radio slogan to advertise a new shampoo for children's hair. Present it to the class.

Write an advertisement telling the class why drugs are bad for you. Use specific examples to back up your opinion.

Compose a jingle (song) for an advertisement about a new kind of gum. (Invent the gum yourself!)

Write a TV advertisement for a new kind of candy bar. Sell it to the class.

Compare and contrast the advertisements for the top two leading soft drinks. Which do you feel is more successful and why?

Create a newspaper advertisement for either a brand-new cologne or perfume. (Invent it yourself!)

Compose a jingle for an advertisement about tennis shoes. Sing it to the class.

Choose any product or invent your own. Then write either a TV, radio, newspaper or magazine advertisement for it. Present it to the class.

Brainstorm all the different ways to make an advertisement, both TV and billboard.

Create a new kind of household product. Then write a magazine advertisement for it.

Interview an individual who works at an ad agency and try to discover what kinds of jobs there are and how much they pay.

Create a magazine advertisement for a tasty kind of ice cream.

Catch This Slogan!

A new brand of computer has just come onto the market. Your job as chief advertiser is to design a magazine and a billboard ad for it. Be creative and think of a catchy slogan. Good luck!

143

GA1321

An Ingenious Telephone

You have invented the greatest kind of telephone ever thought of! You've decided to do your own advertising, so a newspaper ad needs to be made by you. It's a full-page ad and should contain the name of your product, the price, the location, the hours open and if you're having a sale or not. Have fun!

144

A Jingle of a Song

You are working on a radio advertisement and are in need of a catchy jingle or song to play. Come up with a jingle about a new kind of toy.

145

GA1321

A Card Shark or Great White Week

Teacher Tactics

Setting the Stage: Pose the following to your class: "Are any of you afraid of sharks? There's really no need to be as you will soon find out. During Super Shark Week you'll discover the great white shark, the same whom *Jaws* was modeled after. It is only out for prey and not for man. You'll also find out about many other sharks and participate in numerous activities."

"Sharks, literally, must swim for their lives." Ask students to give an explanation of what this might mean and then use the encyclopedia to offer a justified answer.

Create a Shark Jeopardy game using the answers you find about sharks in your shark resources, and then develop the questions the students should ask. You can create a Shark Jeopardy Board out of poster board, index cards and laminating film. It will last for years.

You can order a preserved dogfish shark from Carolina Biological Supply Company or any other biological supply house. Shark dissection guide, shark jaws and shark teeth are also available. These are great for anatomy study, dissection and microscopic scrutiny.

Teaching sharks to an older class opens up the possibility of encouraging them to work with the younger students. After older students learn about the external, internal and eye of the shark, they can create diagrams, flash cards and full-scale pictures to use to teach the younger children. You may even want to include another class as part of your Shark Week.

Set up five centers, two containing microscopes, one of which will contain shark jaws, another shark teeth, another shark denticles, a shark stomach, and if at all possible, order a pregnant female shark and dissect her to display the embryos at the fifth center.

GA1321

A Card Shark or Great White Week

Absolutely Adaptable Activities

Imagine you can talk to a shark. What question(s) would you ask?

What if you caught a shark while you were out fishing? What would you do?

There are about 250 different species of sharks living in oceans all over the world. List as many types as you can.

Sharks have this rather strange habit called feeding frenzy. Describe this strange phenomenon in an informational poem.

The great white shark, "King of the Man-eaters," has some very interesting ancestry. Research the Carcharodon and make an illustrated time line of his prehistoric ancesters.

White sharks can grow to be twenty feet (6.1 m) long and sometimes do attract swimmers. For this reason, the sharks in the *Jaws* series were modeled after the great white shark. Write your own version of *Jaws*, but this time make the shark the hero rather than the villain.

Mako sharks are the swiftest of all sharks and can grow to a length of twelve feet (3.64 m). They devour their prey whole, as entire swordfish, sword and all, have been found in their stomachs. They have a close relative named a porbeagle. Compare and contrast the two on a chart.

The whale shark and the basking shark are the world's biggest fish. Imagine that these two fish can talk and walk but need homes and areas in which to live. Design the habitats for these giant fish and then write a dialogue that these two might have.

Create a large poster which displays pictures of the bull shark, wobbegong, dogfish, Greenland shark, skaamoog, swell shark, goblin shark, lantern shark and frilled shark.

Find out all the similarities and differences between the blue shark and the blue whale and place them into lists.

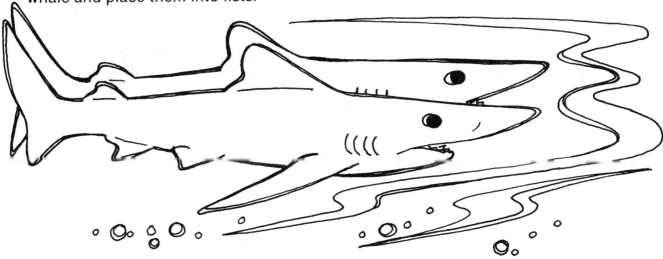

147

GA1321

Labeling Parts of a Shark!

For many years, sharks have been thought of as mindless killers. After much scientific reconsideration, sharks are now determined to be some of the most adapted of all fish and can live in lakes, as well as ocean depths, without much difficulty. Only a very few types have attacked people and that is only after being provoked or in an accidental situation where a human is misunderstood to be prey.

A shark has *pores* on the front of its body to help locate prey. At the other end of its body, it has a *caudal fin* or *tail fin* which is used for swimming. The *dorsal fin(s)* is found along the back.

A shark has two *eyes* which are used to locate prey. It has two *nostrils* which are not used for breathing but rather for smelling.

A shark's *pectoral fins* are located near the gills, and they're used for steering. The *gills* of a shark are used to help a shark breathe by taking oxygen out of the water. The *pelvic fins* are found near the rear of the shark, and they are used for steering too.

Sharks have many, many *teeth* which they use for capturing prey.

Instructions for Students: Carefully study the shark picture below. Use the terms italicized in the above paragraphs to label the picture.

148

GA1321

Dreaming of Sharkomania!

You just had a dream about a shark, but the only things you clearly remember are fins, a boat, safety, a miracle and a bunch of people cheering!

Your job is to fill in the blanks in your memory and write your dream script as incredibly as you can. Good luck and have fun!

149

GA1321

Sharks—Dressed to Kill!

Below are listed ten different sharks and four columns of items for each to wear. Your job is to first look up each of the sharks in your library, sketch a picture of each and then choose various items from each column below and "dress" up the sharks. Make them look as humorous as possible while learning how each one looks in real life first. Have fun!

Shark	Outfit	Accessories	Jewelry	Shoes
lemon	evening gown	sunglasses	rings	sandals
hammerhead	suit	sun visor	bracelet	golf shoes
thresher	jeans	top hat	necklace	tennis shoes
tiger	T-shirt	baseball cap	watch	ballet shoes
goblin	vest	scarf	chain	high heels
mako	bathrobe	tie	pin	flip flops
great white	coat	goggles	button	wedding shoes
whale	shorts	straw hat	earrings	moccasins
basking	kimono	boa	bolo tie	cowboy boots
dogfish	turtleneck	turban	feather	work boots

150

Earthquake Appreciation Week

Teacher Tactics

Setting the Stage: Pose the following to your class: "Have any of you ever been in an earthquake? What was it like? If no one has ever been in an earthquake, what do you think it might be like? This week we'll discover all about earthquakes, the damage they cause, the states most likely to have an earthquake and all about aftershocks and faults."

For free materials about earthquakes ask for (1) World Seismicity and Volcanic Activity in 1975, (2) Volcanoes of the World (a full-color map) and (3) Earthquake Epicenters of the World (a do-it yourself icosahedron globe) when writing to:

>   The United States Dept. of Commerce
>   Nat. Oceanic and Atmospheric Admin.
>   Environmental Data Service
>   Boulder, CO 80302

There have been quite a few major earthquakes in the past around the world. Some on which you may want to have students do research are

>   The Lisbon Earthquake of 1755
>   The Great Alaska Earthquake of 1964
>   The San Francisco Earthquake of 1906
>   The Naples Earthquake of 1857
>   The Assam Earthquake of 1897

Invite someone into the classroom who reads a seismograph, and ask him to share his expertise.

Invite someone into the classroom who has experienced a major earthquake firsthand. Ask him to share his experiences with the class.

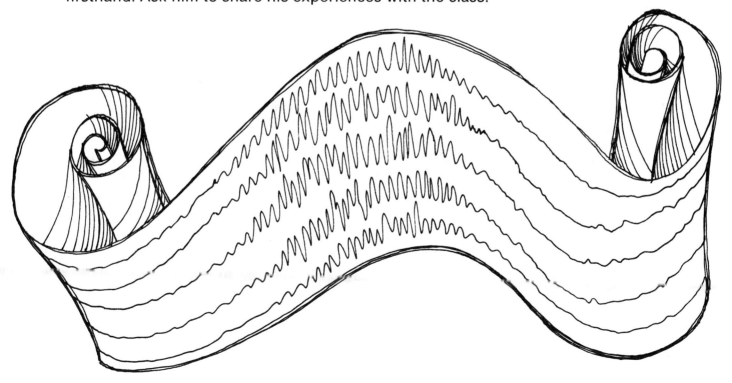

GA1321

Earthquake Appreciation Week

Absolutely Adaptable Activities

Imagine that you are in an earthquake and your building shakes quite a bit. Where would you go for cover?

How would you make your bedroom earthquake-proof?

A violent shaking of the ground may last a minute or two, and it's called an earthquake. What else is as terrifying as an earthquake would be? Make a list.

Make a list of all the things earthquakes can damage.

Sometimes the aftereffects of an earthquake can be more horrifying than the quake itself. Avalanches and tidal waves can also be after the earthquake. Research these natural phenomena and write about what you've discovered.

The crust, mantle and core all play major parts in an earthquake. Look these up and define each.

In an "Earthquake Glossary," give explanations of the following: *seismic waves, focus, body waves, primary waves, secondary waves*.

The epicenter is the spot on the surface of the earth directly over the focus. Think about your town or city. Which point or place would you call the epicenter?

During an earthquake the land may rise in some places, and in other places it may drop. Make a list of all the things that can rise and another list of things that can fall.

Aftershocks can follow strong earthquakes. What kinds of "aftershocks" do people have? After fights? After bankruptcy? After divorce? Think of some on your own.

A fault is a crack in the earth's crust where two sections of the crust have moved. *Fault* means several different things. Look it up in the dictionary and write down the different meanings.

Earthquakes are also caused by the movement of magma within a volcano. Research this type of earthquake and report to your class.

Which states are most likely to have earthquakes? Which other states have also had quakes? I'll give you a hint: Totally, there have been earthquakes in twelve states.

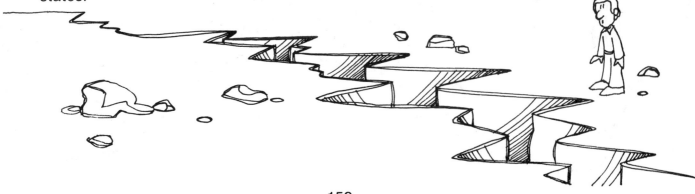

GA1321

Earthquake on the Loose!

Earthquakes can cause some pretty devastating changes, like buildings that move off their foundations or rivers that change course. You are to write a short story about an earthquake that hits your city, and you are right in the middle of it. How are you going to save yourself and your family? How will you save your home and belongings? Be as specific as possible in your story.

153

GA1321

Earthquake-Proof

Design a three-story building which could withstand a major earthquake. In other words, make it earthquake-proof! Show your design in a picture below.

154

GA1321

Surviving an Earthquake

If you knew you lived in a state with a high possibility of having an earthquake, what would you do to make your home and family as safe as possible? List everything you would do before, during and after an earthquake.

155

GA1321

National Library Week

(Begins Third Week of April)

Teacher Tactics

Setting the Stage: Pose the following to your class: "How many of you enjoy reading books? From where do the books you read come? That's right—the library! Well, this is National Library Week and we're going to do a group of activities which relate to library books and the library numerical system—the Dewey Decimal System."

After reading a book to your class, ask students to do the following:

Write a short sequel using the same characters as in the book.

Design folder games where comprehension questions are asked.

Paint a class mural which depicts one or more scenes from the story.

Imagine they are the authors of the book and prepare interviews. Write both the questions and answers they feel the author might give.

In groups, set the story to at least three different kinds of music.

List ten reasons why someone should want to read this book.

Round robin read each sentence of a section or the entire book as it goes around the room.

Create a roll-up movie of the various scenes in the book.

Construct a bulletin board display for the book.

Brainstorm a list of every type of book you can, and then place the books in the Dewey Decimal System.

National Library Week

Absolutely Adaptable Activities

After reading a book do the following:

Pretend the main characters in the story switch roles. How would the story change?

Make predictions of what would happen next if the story were to continue.

Draw a series of cartoons which display the main characters in the different scenes occurring in the story.

Create a puppet show with characters and scenes from the story. Dress the puppets in the same costumes the characters might have worn.

Write a letter to one of the characters telling him/her how you feel about something that happened in the story.

Add or subtract five details from the story. How does it change?

Write a one-paragraph humorous summation of the story.

Construct a diorama depicting a scene from the story and make it out of at least five different mediums.

Add humor to the story.

Reverse or mix up the sequences of events in the book.

Use words or phrases from the story to create a poem.

Create a commercial to sell the book to the class.

Dramatize the book by dressing up like the character and acting out a scene.

Illustrate several pages from the book using your own interpretation.

Name some famous people who might play the part(s) of the book character(s) very well.

Create a secret word search using the names of characters and ideas from the book.

Write ten riddles about the book's characters and scenes.

Compose a tall tale, using the character(s) and story from the book as a basis.

Design a bookmark that shows a scene or character from the book.

157

Dewey, Speak to Me!

000-099 General Works (encyclopedias, magazines, bibliographies)
100-199 Philosophy, Psychology, Ethics
200-299 Religion and Myths
300-399 Sociology (civics, economics, education)
400-499 Philology (language, dictionaries, grammar)
500-599 Science (math, chemistry, biology, botany)
600-699 Useful Arts (medicine, agriculture, TV)
700-799 Fine Arts (painting, music, photography)
800-899 Literature (novels, poetry, plays)
900-999 History, Geography, Biography

Above is the Dewey Decimal System for classification of books. Below are five short paragraphs from five different books. In which of the ten Dewey Decimal categories does each paragraph belong?

1. A beautiful picture was shot over the Grand Canyon last fall. It showed the most beautiful sunset in the background of a gigantic hole. No other picture has even been taken like it.

2. Many algae are microscopic in nature and some float in lakes and oceans. These algae are called phytoplankton. Many marine animals use the algae as a major food source.

3. The Chinese believe in a practice called acupuncture, which means inserting needles into parts of the body to help relieve pain. This was thought to control the flow of Yin and Yang.

4. gander /gan-dar/ n [ME, fr. OE gandra; akin to OE gosgoose] 1: the adult male goose, 2 gander vi, dial: wander, ramble, 3 gander slang: look, glance.

5. Indian, American. Indians were the first people who lived in the Americas. For thousands of years before any one else arrived, they had dwelled there.

GA1321

Cover a Book!

After you have read a book that you find especially exciting, try to imagine what the cover of the book should have looked like. Then draw that new cover below.

GA1321

A Title Is a Title Is a Title!

Below you will find a column of book titles. Your job is to place all the book titles into alphabetical order in the space on the right. Good luck!

Little House on the Prairie

Moby Dick

Nobody Knows!

Are You There God? It's Me, Margaret

Picture This!

Young as a Bee

Reckless Thieves

Snackin' Candy

Christmas Cheer

Freedom Rules!

"InKredible" Kites Week

Teacher Tactics

Setting the Stage: Pose the following to your class: "Have you ever felt bored on a Saturday afternoon? Did you ever wish you could go out to the park and fly a kite? Well, this week we're going to study kites and find out all about them."

Ask the class to write reports on the following questions: What type of kite did Alexander Graham Bell invent? What kite inspired the Wright Brothers to build their first glider? What important discovery did Ben Franklin make while using a kite? What did Marconi do with his kite?

Dangerous experimentation with kites has taken place over the years. Brainstorm with the class what this experimentation might have been.

Arrange for a kite flying tournament in your school. Put out a rule sheet (time involved in getting into the air, etc.) and design ribbons and awards for the winners. There should also be different events and categories set ahead of time.

Kites have served very different purposes over the past years. Have the class brainstorm for what purposes.

What are some of the tools used in kite construction? Assign class members to find out what they are. Call a hardware store and find out the price. Have everyone add them up.

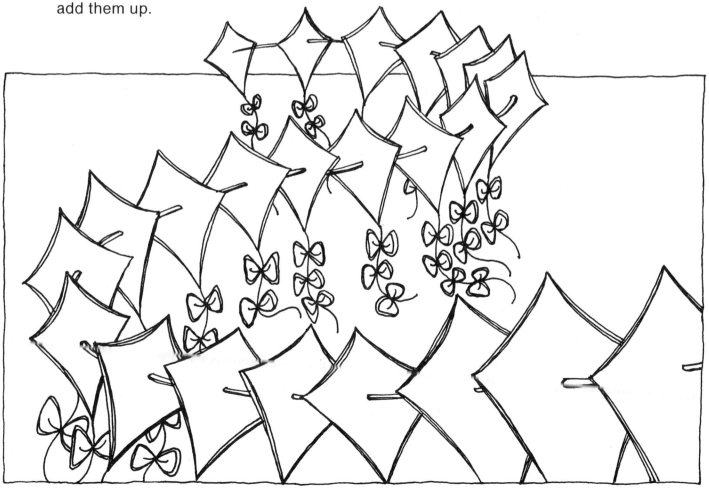

GA1321

"InKredible" Kites Week

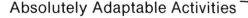

Absolutely Adaptable Activities

You are flying your kite one cloudy afternoon and all of a sudden, lightning flashes! What should you do?

Name five possible causes of failure or reasons why a kite might not fly.

The King of Siam loaded his kites with explosives and sent them over the capital building to regain his throne. For what other selfish reasons might kites have been used?

Kites must possess three qualities—lightness, rigidity and resistance. List/Define each and give an example.

Your kite gets stuck in a tree. How would you get it down?

Name all the dos and don'ts of kite flying in a scroll you share with the class.

What world records have been set with kites? Try the *Guinness Book of World Records* for the answers. Then think of your own ideas to set a world record. Share it with the class.

List five things to do with a kite besides fly it.

Design your own kite, complete with decorations, and construct it yourself. Fly it and see how successful you've been.

Write a weather bulletin which describes a perfect day for kite flying.

List as many different materials as you can think of that can be used to make a kite tail.

A triangular box kite with wings was used by Admiral Byrd's polar expedition. What might have been its intended purpose(s)?

What's the difference between an English kite and a two-stick kite? Look them up and write all their similarities and differences.

Go to the local kite store and make a list of all the different kinds of kites they sell. Design a kite catalogue.

What purpose did kites serve in the Far East? Is this belief true today as well?

Describe the most suitable string for use in kite flying. List the other types of string available, too.

Design a kite logo that bears your name and a distinguishing symbol.

Brainstorm and list all the different decorations that could possibly decorate a kite. Make an art gallery of original pictures which illustrate some of the different decorations.

Imagine you are in charge of a playground where everyone is flying kites. What would be some of the rules?

GA1321

Haiku, We Love You!

Haikus are three-line Japanese poems with the following pattern:
 5 syllables
 7 syllables
 5 syllables

For example:

Kites fly overhead
Some colorful, others bright
Flying in the clouds

Now it's your turn! Write your own haiku about kites. Have fun!

GA1321

Kites Reach New Heights

Copyright © 1991, Good Apple

164

GA1321

All Wasn't Right When I Went to Fly My Kite!

It's a beautiful sunny day and the wind is blowing mildly. You have your rainbow-colored box kite, and you're ready to go to the park. You collect all of your gear, and you're almost out the door when you realize that something's wrong.

What is wrong? Did you leave something behind? Is something wrong in your home? Create something wrong and then finish this story in the first person.

GA1321

Endangered Species Week

Teacher Tactics

Setting the Stage: Pose the following to your class: "Are any of you concerned with the animals that are becoming endangered or even extinct because of what man has done? What are some of the solutions you have for this problem? This week we'll talk about endangered species and what we can do."

You cannot buy a dinosaur. They became extinct 65 million years ago and they won't be back again. A lot of other animals died too and this is called "mass extinction." We're having a kind of mass extinction today, and it's being caused by man. With your class, name at least ten things man can do to stop this current mass extinction of one species a day.

Endangered species are lingering on the edge of extinction this very minute. Name at least twenty endangered animals with your class.

Find a video in your public library showing endangered species. Share it with your class and then discuss it. Design a quiz or fact sheet to accompany it.

Some topics for reports on endangered animals include the Gila trout, American crocodile, American alligator, Eastern cougar, black-footed ferret, manatee, gray wolf, red wolf, California condor, whooping crane, bald eagle, brown pelican, catfish, gorilla, leopard, ocelot, orangutan, Asian elephant, tiger, Bactrian camel, eight species of whales, twelve species of monkeys and the Japanese crane.

GA1321

Endangered Species Week

Absolutely Adaptable Activities

Energy is the force that living organisms need to survive. Name as many things that possess energy as you can.

An environment along with the organisms that live in it is called an ecosystem. Name one ecosystem with all its parts.

Some people believe that by hunting the rhinoceros, they can use the body parts to cure diseases or even, believe it or not, help to improve their love lives. These people kill the rhino mercilessly and the poor rhinoceros hasn't a chance. Write an editorial to these rhino hunters stating how you feel about what they're doing.

Endangered animals have difficulty staying alive for one reason or another. Unless something is done fairly quickly, endangered animals may die out or become extinct. For instance, the polar bear, leopard and giraffe are all on the endangered species list. Think of three ways to help stop these animals from dying out.

Many animals eat specific types of plants and when the plants die out, so do the animals. One example of this is the giant panda bear eating his bamboo. When the bamboo dies out, and it has on several occasions, whole groups of pandas die. Some estimate there are only 300 pandas left both in the wild and in captivity. Look up giant pandas and write down nine facts about them.

Animals need homes, just like people do. Name at least ten different animal homes.

Habitats are the food, water, space and air that makes an animal able to live comfortably. Every animal has its own individual habitat. For instance, a lizard has its territory and that's its space, it catches small insects and that's its food, rainwater serves as its water source and there's plenty of air to go around. Try to discover three animals and their four-part habitats.

Animals are hunted for many different reasons. Make a list of every reason you can think why man might hunt a certain animal.

Write to government officials about endangered animals and tell them how you feel.

Pretend you are a TV news reporter. Interview a hunter to see how he/she feels about endangered species. What would you ask?

Write How You Feel!

Write a letter below about your feelings regarding endangered species and send it to one of these three agencies:

National Wildlife Federation
1412 16th St., N.W.
Washington, D.C. 20036

Defenders of Wildlife
1244 Nineteenth St., N.W.
Washington, D.C. 20036

Rare Animal Relief Effort
c/o National Audobon Society
950 Third Ave.
New York, NY 10022

168

Tell It Like It Is!

Pretend that a person from another planet came to live on earth and was interested in endangered animals. Try to explain to him everything you know about why animals have come to be endangered and what solutions man has found. Be as specific as possible.

169

Add the Endangered Animals

a.   9 California condors
   + 2 hooded parakeets
      endangered birds

b.   7 humpback whales
   + 3 sperm whales
      endangered whales

c.   4 snow leopards
   + 5 Siberian tigers
      endangered big cats

d.   6 African elephants
   + 2 Asian elephants
      endangered elephants

e.   3 giant otters
   + 9 hawksbill turtles
      endangered sea animals

f.   2 American alligators
   + 4 American crocodiles
      endangered reptiles

g.   8 Javan rhinoceros
   + 7 Northern square-lipped rhinos
      endangered rhinos

h.   8 Fiji banded iguanas
   + 6 Komodo dragons
      endangered lizards

i.   5 Central Asian cobras
   + 9 Burmese pythons
      endangered snakes

j.   7 Douc langurs
   + 6 proboscis monkeys
      endangered monkeys

k.   3 bald eagles
   + 8 Wagler's macaws
      endangered birds

l.   2 red uakaris
   + 6 drills
      endangered monkeys

m.   9 Spanish lynxes
   + 7 Asiatic lions
      endangered big cats

n.   10 gaurs
   + 7 Asiatic buffalo
      endangered oxen

GA1321

Johnny Appleseed Week

Teacher Tactics

Setting the Stage: Pose the following to your class: "Does anyone in here like apples? Have you ever examined an apple up close? Did you ever wonder how apple trees got all over the United States? You're going to discover all about Johnny Appleseed and his walk across the country."

Make or create an apple dish with your class. (Examples: Apple Brown Betty, Apple Crisp, Apple Tarts, Applesauce, etc.)

Teach your class the parts of the apple flower or apple blossom, which can be found in any book on apples or encyclopedia.

Try to find several of each of the following types of apples to show to your class: Red Delicious, Golden Delicious, Rome Beauty, MacIntosh and Jonathan. Cut them up and give one piece of each type to each student. Then write the five types across the top of your chalkboard, and solicit adjectives to describe the five. Also, keep one whole apple of each type so they can also describe how they look.

Visit an apple orchard with your class.

Collect apples and dissect one or more to observe under a microscope.

Two good books for children are *Johnny Appleseed* by Carol Beach York and *The Story of Johnny Appleseed* by Aliki Brandenberg.

Johnny Appleseed Week

Absolutely Adaptable Activities

In her book *Apples, Apples, Apples,* Elizabeth Helfman tells how apples are harvested, and "a clear, dry day was best for picking. First the apple helpers stood on the ground and picked into baskets all the apples they could reach. Then up into the trees they went on ladders. The highest apples were reached with a 'picker,' a long pole with a wire basket on the end." Brainstorm all the ways to pick apples that you can think of.

Eat an apple and describe how it looks, smells, tastes and feels.

Name all the things that can be made from apples.

In stories of the past, and folktales, there was a certain magic about apples. If you ate a specific apple, you could live forever. Sometimes if you possessed three gold apples, you received magic, but they were not to be eaten. An apple at the end of the world could save the dying royalty. The apples in these stories went on and on. Write three or four of your own apple tales of magic.

Think about the story of Snow White and the wicked witch and the poison apple. Write your own version of the story and make sure there is an apple somewhere in it.

A fruit called an elephant apple grows in the East Indies and eastern Asia. It is the size of a large apple, but the flesh is brown and not sweet. This is really not an apple at all. How many other fruits are named one thing but are really something else?

Another name for New York City is "the Big Apple." There are Big Apple neckties, T-shirts, shopping bags, napkins and buttons, just to mention a few. Brainstorm all the other paraphenalia (items) that could relate to the "Big Apple."

The most famous apple grower never did stay put on any one area of land. His name was John Chapman, better known as Johnny Appleseed, whose mission was to make sure every farm in the Middle West had apple trees. He gathered bagfuls of apple seeds and planted them wherever he found an open field. He was welcome everywhere and everyone knew the name of Johnny Appleseed. Research more about John Chapman and write an eight-line poem about what you find.

Make a list of all the kitchen gadgets that are used to work with apples.

There are at least five different varieties of apples. Research what they are and name them.

An Apple by Any Other Name . . .

In the years before the Civil War, several new varieties of apples were discovered and grown. The names that were given to these different kinds of apples included Seek-No-Further, Missing Link and Sweet Maiden's Blush, just to name a few.

Different labels for apple packages were invented. Below you are to create two labels for apple crates. You may invent the name of the apples, too.

GA1321

Apple Blossom Bingo

Below is a picture of an apple blossom. Please label all the parts from the words in the box. If you need help, use the encyclopedia or a book on apples.

pollen grains	stigma	style
anther	ovule	filament

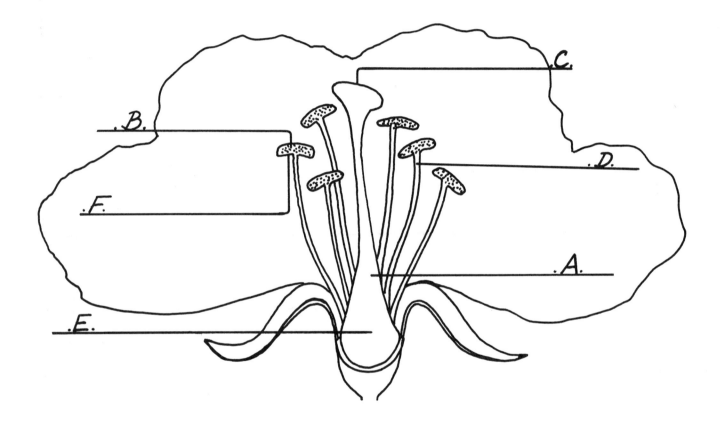

A. _____
B. _____
C. _____
D. _____
E. _____
F. _____

GA1321

Apple Tale

Many fairy tales have been told over the years with the topic of "apples" in them. On this page, you are to write a fairy tale of your own which focuses on apples. Use as many facts as you know about apples in your story.

Plane Talk Week

Teacher Tactics

Setting the Stage: Pose the following to your class: "How many of you have ever been up in an airplane? How about a helicopter? What was it like? This week we'll learn all about airplanes, who invented them, and all the ways life would be different without them."

The Italian Leonardo da Vinci originally thought of it in 1500. The Englishman Sir George Cayley invented it in 1804. The American Wright Brothers first flew it on December 17, 1903, at Kitty Hawk, North Carolina. Hold a class discussion to see how much your students know already, and then assign research reports to each class member to fill in the holes. Later, hold another class discussion and determine who these men were and what they did.

Turn your class into a "flying" airplane! Make a blueprint showing the major airplane parts, as well as the furniture and accessories in the classroom. Then set the room up just like the interior of a passenger airplane. Have students board the plane and simulate a real ride from one location to another. Make up tickets and students have to find their seats. Assign a captain/pilot, copilot, stewardesses and attendants. If you're studying an area in social studies, use landmarks that they can imagine they're seeing out the "windows."

Visit a local air museum or airport to view the sights, preferably with a tour guide. Hold a class discussion after the field trip.

GA1321

Plane Talk Week

Absolutely Adaptable Activities

A popular song says: "Fly me to the moon, and let me dream among the stars. . . ." Write your own set of lyrics to complete this song.

Design your own airplane and then create a model of it.

Before airplanes had been invented, men often thought that if they constructed birdlike wings, attached them to a man's arms and flapped that they would be able to fly. Name five creative ways that you might think of to be able to fly if there was no such thing as airplanes.

The invention of the airplane was truly a great accomplishment, and one which many take for granted today. Write a short essay about how you feel in regard to man flying in airplanes.

Brainstorm all the things you can think of which can fly.

Prior to the Wright Brothers inventing the airplane, they were bicycle makers and mechanics. Combine an airplane with a bicycle in a drawing.

Because the Wright Brothers put patents on every part of their flying machine and were very careful people who wanted to take the time to perfect their craft, their strategy stopped improvement and development of aircraft in America. Thus, European individuals stormed ahead in the development of the airplane. Do you feel the Wright Brothers were right or wrong for keeping their discoveries to themselves? Write an essay stating what you think and give your reasons.

The airplane progressed from the flapping wings to the helicopters to the hot air balloons to the airplane. Draw a picture of each one of these in a flow chart.

Imagine living in the days before there were airplanes. How would life be different? Make a list of ways.

Write all the words that rhyme with *plane.*

Research Leonardo da Vinci and the part he played with the airplane.

Sir George Cayley, the Father of Aviation, created the convertiplane, a combination of a helicopter and airplane. Combine an airplane and a hot air balloon, an airplane and a go-cart and an airplane and a clock. Draw each one.

Write an eight-line poem relaying your feelings about airplanes.

The Wright Brothers and others early in aviation were ridiculed for doing something so "ridiculous." If you were trying to invent something brand-new that had never been thought of before and people were making fun of you, would you continue? Write a one-half-page essay with your answer.

GA1321

What Can It Mean?

Look up the following terms about airplanes in a book, encyclopedia or dictionary. As you do, learn what they mean!

Aerodynamics:

Biplane:

Dual-control system:

Fuselage:

Jet engine:

Monoplane:

Rocket:

Vacuum:

Wind tunnel:

GA1321

101 Days in the Air

Imagine that you had to spend a very long time in an airplane. Pretend that some very remarkable things happened while you were in the air. Write a short adventure story entitled "101 Days in Flight."

179

GA1321

Master of the Universe

Combine the wings of an airplane, the body of a boat and the tracks of a tank and create a new "Master of the Universe" machine! Make a detailed diagram of both the interior and the exterior. Have fun!

GA1321

Super Spindly Spider Week

Teacher Tactics

Setting the Stage: Pose the following to your class: "Is anyone afraid of spiders? Do you have any idea of how many different kinds of spiders there are? Most spiders are harmless to man, as we'll discover during Super Spindly Spider Week. Spiders are web makers and all spiders spin silk. You'll learn much more."

Visit a museum for arachnids with your class, and ask students to carry clipboards and draw pictures of the different spiders as they go along. Then, upon returning to the classroom, go over the different spider species and assign them as topics for students to study.

Ask an expert on spiders, or even possibly a pet store owner, to come and speak to your class about spiders. Have interview questions ready prior to the visit and go over them while he/she is there.

Here is a list of spiders for research topics: tarantula, white lady spider, a baboon spider, trap-door spider, crab spider, woodlouse killer, raft spider, garden spider, daddy longlegs spider, bird-eating spider, lynx spider and water spider.

Create identification charts using the names of various spiders and associating them with the section of the world where they live. A good resource for this is *First Sight Spiders* by Lionel Bender, Aladdin Books, Ltd.

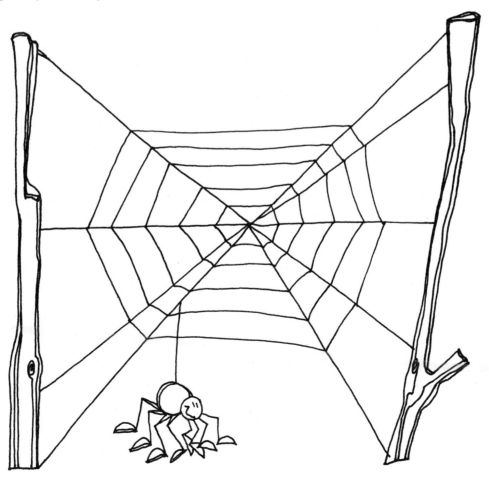

GA1321

Super Spindly Spider Week

Absolutely Adaptable Activities

Draw a picture of a giant spiderweb.

Spiders are eight-legged creatures called arachnids, and they come in all shapes and sizes both small and large. Name anything you can think of which also relates to the number eight.

All spiders spin webs of silk. Research silk and make a list of all its uses.

Although all spiders have fangs which they inject into their prey to kill it, only a few spiders would ever harm people. Look *spiders* up in the encyclopedia and try to discover which are the spiders that are harmful to man.

Draw a picture of a tarantula.

The actual act of spinning a web is a very curious process. Make a step-by-step direction sheet, from the time the spider bridges the gap to when it completes the sticky spiral.

A spider's silk is very strong. It can even hold up a very large spider with no problem. Name things that in the world of humans are equally as strong.

Spiders spin silk for many different reasons. Make a list of those reasons.

Research how the wolf spider and nursery-web spider deal with their babies. Do they carry them on their bodies, do they bury them, do they lay them on the ground or what do they do?

There are also many different kinds of web makers: orb weavers, sheet web weavers and hammock weavers. Find out as much as you can about all three of these types of web makers.

There are solitary (live alone) spiders and communal (live with many) spiders. In human life can you think of any solitary men or women?

Research black widows and the brown recluse. What do they have in common? What is different?

Some spiders build webs while others are hunting spiders. Make a list of all the spiders you can find in books that fall under each category.

Spiders can take food in liquid form. Name all the liquids you can think of.

Pretend you are a spider. You get the choice of where to go. Where would you choose?

Space-Going Spiders

In Norman Barrett's book *Spiders,* it was noted that in the 1970's, some experiments were conducted by U.S. high school students and carried out in *Skylab,* the space laboratory orbiting in space. One of the experiments was to find out whether the lack of gravity had any effect on the web-spinning ability of spiders. Two garden spiders, Anita and Arabella, were studied and the final conclusion was that the webs they spun in space were irregular.

Design a commemorative stamp that honors spiders in space.

GA1321

A Spider Myth

A Greek myth is told about a small girl, Arachne, who was changed into a spider for trying to challenge the goddess Athene to a tapestry-weaving contest, and she was therefore doomed to spin forever from that moment on.

Write your own myth, and make sure there is some mention of a spider in it.

GA1321

Spider Time Subtraction

a. 9 tarantulas
    − 2
    ———————
    tarantulas

b. 7 baboon spiders
    − 4
    ———————
    baboon spiders

c. 8 crab spiders
    − 3
    ———————
    crab spiders

d. 6 jumping spiders
    − 5
    ———————
    jumping spiders

e. 5 wolf spiders
    − 2
    ———————
    wolf spiders

f. 9 lynx spiders
    − 5
    ———————
    lynx spiders

g. 8 garden spiders
    − 4
    ———————
    garden spiders

h. 4 raft spiders
    − 2
    ———————
    raft spiders

i. 6 water spiders
    − 3
    ———————
    water spiders

j. 5 trap-door spiders
    − 1
    ———————
    trap-door spiders

k. 9 white lady spiders
    − 7
    ———————
    white lady spiders

l. 8 daddy longlegs
    − 4
    ———————
    daddy longlegs

m. 3 bird-eating spiders
    − 2
    ———————
    bird-eating spiders

n. 6 yellow crab spiders
    − 4
    ———————
    yellow crab spiders

Women in "Herstory" Week

Teacher Tactics

Setting the Stage: Pose the following to your class: "There have been many women in history who have made an impact on the world as we know it today. Some of these women aren't commonly known and that's why this week, Women in 'Herstory' will tell 'her story' as we now know it."

Assign each student to do research on a famous woman in history. Select any courageous women you can think of. Some examples are Anne Hutchinson, Abigail Adams, Dolley Madison, Narcissa Whitman, Julia Ward Howe, Susan B. Anthony, Dorothea Lynde Dix, Mary Lyon, Ida M. Tarbell and Eleanor Roosevelt.

These women are known for their contributions in the area of science: Margaret Mead, Dixie Lee Ray, Chien Shiung Wu, Elizabeth Shull Russell and Charlotte Friend. Ask students to discover the area of science in which each woman excels and find out a little more about each one's accomplishments.

Invite a woman leader from your local community to come to speak with your class. Impress upon your class prior to her visit why she is considered a leader and why it has been so hard for so long for women to take the stand with men— equality in job and home and in politics, government and business.

Create a giant class collage of drawings and cutouts of women whom the class considers to be "great." Make sure they're prepared to back up their choices.

GA1321

Women in "Herstory" Week

Absolutely Adaptable Activities

Nellie Bly was called the first Woman of the News. Try to discover why she was given this title.

Florence Nightingale was a famous nurse in the Crimean War. Interview a modern day nurse to determine how much influence Ms. Nightingale has today. Report back to the class on "A Day in the Life of a Nurse."

Clara Barton founded the first Red Cross. Telephone the local Red Cross to find out what kinds of services the Red Cross provides. Ask if one of the employees would be willing to come and share with your class.

It took a long time for women to gain the right to vote, and Susan B. Anthony was monumental in achieving this task. Compose a biographical poem about Ms. Anthony's life and her struggles with the politics of primarily men.

Amelia Earhart was the first woman pilot to cross the Atlantic. Make ten possible diary entries prior to, during and after that historical flight. Describe what some of her feelings, fears and thoughts might have been.

Harriet Tubman was a leader in the Underground Railroad during the Civil War. Research this important American to discover just exactly what she did and write a folktale in her honor.

Either draw or cut out pictures of modern day female heroines that you admire. Make a collage.

The first American flag was made by a woman named Betsy Ross. Create a filmstrip (by bleaching out an old one with Clorox and drawing on it with magic marker) showing the class why this was such an historical event.

Do you admire any grown-up woman? What has she done that you think is so wonderful? Write a short paper about her.

Madame Marie Curie worked with her husband to isolate radium and to complete other scientific research. In an oral report, outline her accomplishments.

Annie Oakley was a famous sharpshooter and performer, and a movie was named after her entitled *Annie Get Your Gun.* Why was it so unusual for a woman to be able to "shoot" in those days?

There was only one woman pharaoh in ancient Egypt and her name was Hatshepsut. Compose an imaginary story about what it must have felt like for Hatshepsut in an all-male dominated society.

We have a lot of women in the news business today. Call a local TV or radio station and interview one of the newswomen to discover what it was like getting the job, how they are treated, etc.

GA1321

Sacred Indian Grounds

A young Indian girl named Pocahontas did a very brave thing a long, long time ago. She saved a white man named Captain John Smith from death at the Indian's hand. In doing this, she helped to bring peace between the white man and the Indians.

Imagine that you are a young Indian child back in 1617 and a white man has tried to enter your hunting grounds, which are sacred. How would you respond? Write a story telling about your feelings and your actions.

188

Another Hymn

Julia Ward Howe wrote the song "The Battle Hymn of the Republic" in order to help in the fight for truth, freedom and to end slavery. Write your own song which tells about those things you feel strongest.

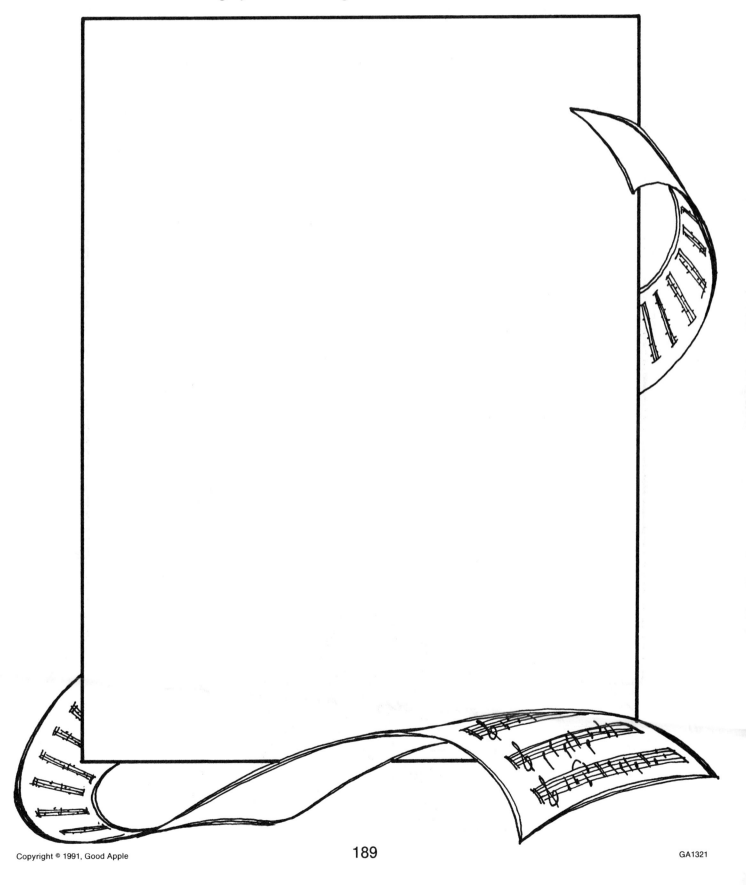

GA1321

Helping the Poor

Jane Addams built a place called Hull House around the early 1900's. She had it built because she had a dream of a big house where the doors could always stay open and people could come and get food and shelter and warmth and understanding. She really wanted to help the poor and through Hull House, she did.

Brainstorm all the ways that you and your city can help the poor and homeless. Make a list.

GA1321

Seal-a-riffic Week

Teacher Tactics

Setting the Stage: Pose the following to your class: "Can you think of an animal who is slippery, has whiskers, can use its flippers to clap hands and lives in the ocean? That's right, a seal! This week we'll be studying seals, sea lions, walruses and their habits."

Ask students to complete research reports on any of the following: Steller sea lion, California sea lion, South American sea lion, Australia sea lion and Hooker's sea lion.

Pinniped means "fin-footed" and three different families of creatures share the finned feet—the sea lions (otariids), seals (phocids) and the walrus (odobenid). With your class, complete a compare-contrast chart for the three families on the chalkboard.

With your students, define the following terms: *bull, cow, migration, molt, nurse, pinniped, predator, pup* and *tide pool.*

If a marine mammal park is close by, visit it with your class. Observe seals, sea lions and walruses. If a field trip is not possible, try to find a video about marine mammals. Discuss what they've seen when you return to the classroom or after viewing the video.

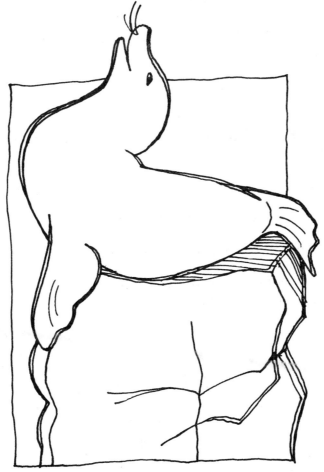

GA1321

Seal-a-riffic Week

Absolutely Adaptable Activities

Design a sea lion glossary, complete with a detailed description for each of the five major types of sea lions.

Rhyme the word *seal* with all the words you can.

Pinniped means "fin-footed," and three different families of creatures share finned feet—the seal, the sea lion and the walrus. How many other creatures have fins? Make a list.

On a poster, illustrate four of the eighteen different types of seals. Write a brief description under each.

Seals which have no external ears are sometimes called true seals. True seals are the largest and most widespread of the pinniped families. List some uses that man has for these seals.

Design an invitation for a party whose guest star is a seal!

The seal, although it spends a lot of its time in the water, is in fact a mammal and needs to breathe air. Research and list all the other mammals who spend a large amount of their time in the water.

Seals can control their breathing rate in order that they may stay underwater for up to twenty minutes at a time. Imagine that humans had the same ability. How would things change?

Seals cry the blues—a lot! Why is this so?

The elephant seal can grow up to twenty feet (6.1 m) in length and weigh up to 8000 pounds (3600 kg). Compare and contrast this animal with an Asian or an African land elephant.

Make two lists—one of all the seals' uses and one of all of man's uses for blubber.

What are some of the different purposes for a seal's flippers?

A seal's teeth are similar to trees in what way? Report to the class.

Seals, walruses and sea lions are natural-born swimmers. Design and illustrate at least ten different kinds of sea life.

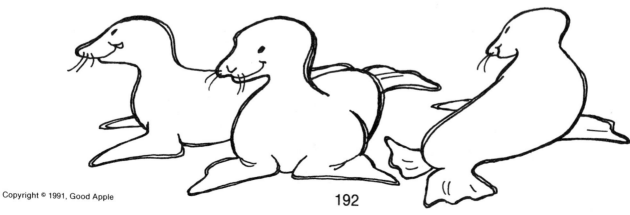

192

GA1321

A Seal Song

The elephant seal, the ribbon seal and the hooded seal are very unique and unusual. Compose the lyrics or words to a song about one, two or all three of these seals.

GA1321

A Seal's Sense of Smell

Seals have a difficult time finding their babies on a crowded beach, simply by looking. So the seals use their excellent sense of smell to identify others.

Imagine you had only your sense of smell and that your other senses didn't work. How would your life be different? Write a poem counting the ways.

194

GA1321

Whiskers Whisk Away

The bearded seal and the walrus use their whiskers to help them search for food on the bottom of the ocean.

Create several other uses for whiskers.

Answer Key

Mix 'Em Up, Page 23: 1. limestone 2. quartz 3. feldspar 4. granite 5. topaz 6. emerald 7. mica 8. pyrite 9. turquoise 10. marble

A Gem of a Story Problem, Page 24: 1. 78 (35.1 kg) 2. 77 (34.65 kg) 3. 63 (28.35 kg) 4. 107 (48.15 kg) total = 325 (146.25 kg) avg. = 81.25 (36.56 kg)

Monster's Yard Sale, Page 49: $90 + $50 + $30 + $80 + $10 + $20 + $70 + $40 + $60 = $450

Monster Scramble, Page 50: 1. Cyclops 2. Loch Ness 3. Big Foot 4. Abominable Snowman 5. Headless Horseman 6. Sea Serpent 7. King Kong 8. Frankenstein

Bicycle Math Marathon, Page 53: 4 + 10 + 23 + 12 + 17 − 2 + 29 + 3 = 96

Wild West Matchup, Page 59: 1. e 2. f 3. i 4. a or g 5. k 6. b 7. d 8. c 9. l 10. h 11. a or g 12. j 13. m

The James Gang's Problem, Page 60: Steven's = $25, Frank's = $50, Jesse's = $75

Heart Multiplication, Page 80: a. 2142 b. 2457 c. 1491 d. 3182 e. 5734 f. 1357 g. 5032 h. 2142 i. 4356 j. 396 k. 4752 l. 1691

Christmas Multiplication, Page 83: a. 536 b. 498 c. 210 d. 364 e. 553 f. 288 g. 87 h. 114 i. 459 j. 288 k. 441 l. 112 m. 116 n. 435

A Potpourri of Thinking Activities, Page 94: 1. 29 critters 3. 44.5 feet (13.56 m)

Monkey Math, Page 98: a. 12 b. 6 c. 15 d. 7 e. 13 f. 11 g. 6 h. 12 i. 16 j. 8 k. 9 l. 11 m. 15 n. 13

Money, Moola, Cash, Stash!, Page 103: 1. $6.50 2. $14.95 3. yes $1.50 4. $3.00

The Family That Borrows, Page 105: $3.35

How Much Is That Invention in the Window?, Page 110: 1. 74 parts 2. 68 supplies 3. $8.16 4. $66.91

Presidential Trivia, Page 123: 1. Ford 2. Taft (6', 300 lbs.) 3. W.H. and B. Harrison 4. Buchanan 5. John Adams and Hoover 6. Nixon 7. John Adams and Jefferson 8. Teddy Roosevelt (42) 9. Jefferson, John Adams and Monroe 10. Reagan (73)

A Ship's Day—Find the Answer!, Page 135: 1. shipping 2. pirates 3. ships 4. galleys 5. rigging 6. clip 7. compound 8. bow 9. stern 10. helm

Double-Digit Dinosaurs, Page 139: a. 72 b. 112 c. 93 d. 126 e. 109 f. 130 g. 107 h. 81 i. 93 j. 131 k. 30 l. 120 m. 65 n. 78

Dewey, Speak to Me!, Page 158: 1. Fine Arts 2. Science 3. Useful Arts 4. Philology 5. General Works

A Title Is a Title Is a Title!, Page 160: *Are You There God?, Christmas Cheer, Freedom Rules!, Little House on the Prairie, Moby Dick, Nobody Knows!, Picture This!, Reckless Thieves, Snackin' Candy, Young as a Bee*

Add the Endangered Animals, Page 170: a. 11 b. 10 c. 9 d. 8 e. 12 f. 6 g. 15 h. 14 i. 14 j. 13 k. 11 l. 8 m. 16 n. 17

Apple Blossom Bingo, Page 174: a. style b. pollen grains c. stigma d. filament e. ovule f. anther

Spider Time Subtraction, Page 185: a. 7 b. 3 c. 5 d. 1 e. 3 f. 4 g. 4 h. 2 i. 3 j. 4 k. 2 l. 4 m. 1 n. 2

Photography, Page 14:

King, Page 89:

GA1321

Bibliography

Anderson, J.I. *I Can Read About Johnny Appleseed.* Troll Association, 1977.

Barrett, Norman. *Spiders.* Franklin Watts, 1989.

Bartlett, John. *Familiar Quotations.* Little, Brown, and Company, 1980.

Bender, Lionel. *Spiders.* Aladdin Books, Ltd.

Boyne, Walter J., *The Smithsonian Book of Flight for Young People.* Antheneum, 1988.

Brandenberg, Aliki. *The Story of Johnny Appleseed.* Simon & Schuster, Inc., 1963.

Burchard, Peter. *Pioneers of Flight.* St. Martin's Press, Inc., 1970.

Coombs, Roy, and Nicholas DeVere. *The Book of Fantastic Planes.* Golden Press, 1974.

Corwin, Judith H. *Christmas Fun.* Simon & Schuster, Inc., 1982.

Crosby, Alexander. *Tarantulas.* Walker and Company, 1981.

Daugherty, Sonia. *The Brave Women.* J. B. Lippincott Company, 1953.

Deur, Lynne. *Doers and Dreamers.* Lerner Publications Company, 1972.

Elting, Mary. *Aircraft at Work.* 1964.

Elwood, Ann, Carol Orsag, and Sidney Solomon. *Macmillan Illustrated Almanac for Kids.* Aladdin Books, Ltd., 1981.

Fowler, Virginia. *Christmas, Crafts, and Customs Around the World.* Simon & Schuster, Inc., 1984.

Gaskin, John. *The Heart.* Franklin Watts, 1985.

Gemming, Elizabeth and Klaus. *Born in a Barn.* 1974.

Guinness Book of World Records. 1987.

Hamma, Elizabeth, and Vickie Hunter. *Stagecoach Days.* Lane Book Company, 1963.

Hannum, Dotti. *A Visit to the Fire Station.* Children's Press, 1985.

Harris, Susan. *Gems and Minerals.* 1980.

Helfman, Elizabeth. *Apples, Apples, Apples.* Thomas Nelson, Inc., Publishers, 1977.

Hollander, Zander, and David Schultz. *Illustrated Sports Record Book.* 1987.

Holling, Holling C. *Book of Cowboys.* The Platt and Munk Company, Inc.

Johnson, Hasannah Lyons. *From Apple Seed to Applesauce.* Lothrop, Lee and Shepard Company, 1977.

Johnson, Sylvia A. *Apple Trees.* Lerner Publications Company, 1983.

Lambert, David. *Earthquakes.* Franklin Watts, 1982.

_____. *Earthquakes and Volcanoes.* Bookwright Press, 1986.

Lampton, Christopher. *Endangered Species.* An Impact Book, 1988.

Levenson, Dorothy. *Women of the West.* Franklin Watts, 1973.

Lisken, Tom. *Nelli Bly: First Woman of the News.* Contemporary Perspectives, Inc., 1978.

McCall, Kedith. *Pirates and Privateers.* Children's Press, 1980.

McGowen, Tom. *Album of Sharks.* 1977.

GA1321

McWilliams, Karen. *Pirates.* Franklin Watts, 1989.

Newman, Dana. *The New Teacher's Almanac.* The Center for Applied Research in Education, Inc., 1980.

Nixon, Hershell, and Joan L. Nixon. *Earthquakes: Native in Motion.* A Skylight Book, 1981.

Noble, Iris. *Contemporary Women Scientists of America.* Julian Messner, 1979.

Pascall, Jeremy. *Pirates and Privateers.* Theorem Publishing, Ltd., 1978.

Pitcher, Caroline—Consultant. *Christmas.* Aladdin Books, Ltd.

Podendorf, Illa. *Rocks and Minerals.* 1982.

Prelutsky, Jack. *The New Kid on the Block.* Greenwillow Books, 1984.

_____. *Ride a Purple Pelican.* Greenwillow Books, 1986.

Rosenfeld, Arthur. *Exotic Pet Book.* Fireside Books, 1987.

Roy, Ron. *What Has Ten Legs and Eats Corn Flakes?* Clarion Books, 1982.

Sechrist, Elizabeth H., and Janette Woolsey. *It's Time for Christmas.* 1959.

Shaffer, Paul, and Herbert Zim. *Rocks and Minerals.* 1957.

Soule, Gardner. *Mystery Monsters of the Deep.* 1981.

Squire, Dr. Ann. *101 Questions and Answers About Pets and People.* Macmillan, 1988.

Steiner, Barbara A. *Biography of a Polar Bear.* 1972.

Stephen, R.J. *Fire Engines.* Franklin Watts, 1986.

Stone, Melissa. Moments in American History Series: *Creative Days. Brighter Tomorrows. You Don't Own Me. Rebellion's Song. Flying High. Larger Than Life. A Cry for Action. Clouds of War. Risking It All.* Steck-Vaughn Company, 1989.

Sullivan, George. *Understanding Photography.* 1972.

Thompson, Brenda, and Rosemary Giesen. *Famous Planes.* 1977.

Van Rose, Susanna. *Earthquakes.* Her Majesty's Stationery Office for the Institute of Geological Sciences, 1983.

Vignati, Giorgio. *Ships.* 1973.

Wallace, Joseph. *The Rise and Fall of the Dinosaur.* Gallery Books, 1987.

Ward, Brian R. *The Heart and Blood.* Franklin Watts, 1982.

Webster, David. *Photo Fun.* 1973.

Weston, Graham. *In the Air.* 1983.

Williams, Brenda. *Fighting a Fire.* Kingfisher Books Ltd., 1987.

World Book Encyclopedia A-Z. 1985.

York, Carol Beach. *Johnny Appleseed.* Troll Association, 1980.

Zoobooks Series: *Gorillas, The Apes, Orangutans, Bears, Polar Bears.* San Diego, California.